Praise for *Figuring It Out*

"*Figuring it Out,* by Libby Connolly Alexander, provides guidance on how to succeed in business through personal persistence, determination, and appropriate risk-taking, combined with hiring and inspiring a talented executive team. Add to this Connolly's formula for creating a winning culture and having a sixth sense for recognizing and capitalizing on the ever-changing world of business, and the reader will have a blueprint for profitably growing a company. The lessons learned are as good as any found in a Harvard business school case study."

—**Jack K. Gelman,** *group chairman, Vistage International, and executive-in-residence, Christopher Newport University, Luter School of Business*

"In days when 'unicorn' companies rise to multi-billion-dollar valuations in a short period of time, only to eventually fall way short of their goals, Larry and Libby Connolly have shown us that the old-fashioned ways of building a multi-billion-dollar business sometimes work the best. Hard work, ingenuity, integrity, and persistence were the key ingredients to the formula that made Connolly such a success story. Libby's story also shows us how a leader who puts the goals of the company ahead of her own personal ambitions will be able to lead a company for the long haul and create outstanding results.

"For those of us who had the chance to work with Libby, we got the opportunity to learn from a truly talented and high-integrity leader. Those who read *Figuring It Out* will take away many invaluable lessons that will help improve the performance of any business."

—**Douglas Present,** *former chairman of the board, Connolly Inc., and Advent International operating partner*

"I had the good fortune to be the chairman of Cotiviti for nearly four years. During this time, Libby was the vice chair. Knowing that Libby had grown up in the Connolly family business, I was consistently impressed with her ability to take a step back from the business she knew so well and apply the virtues of welcoming change, to 'just figure it out' in terms of what was right for the customers and the employees, always with a great deal of humility. Her father clearly was a great coach and role model!"

—**David L. Swift,** *former chairman of Cotiviti, and current chairman and CEO of Serta Simmons Bedding*

"While I worked for Target, I was a client of Libby's, and I can attest to the fact that Connolly was a 'premium brand' and received stellar survey scores from me and my staff. I was responsible for approving the decision to promote Connolly to our primary audit firm, and I made that decision because of their client service, honesty, integrity, and ability to adapt quickly to a rapidly changing environment. Many leaders strive to embed these traits in their company, but few make it happen in reality. Libby's story is a great, real-life example of why this is so important for success!"

—**Melissa Norton,** *CFO, Emoticard Inc.; former senior director, Target Corporation*

"*Figuring It Out* provides an interesting story of a personal and business journey. Libby provides tremendous personal insight on how to make the difficult decisions necessary to build and grow a business, as well as the steps required to achieve strong organizational performance. A great read!"

—**Ken Goulet,** *former board director of Cotiviti, and EVP of Anthem, Inc.*

"First let's describe Libby ... demanding, seeking top performance along with a strong desire to win. This was accomplished in an environment of trust without fear. This was the key. Libby encouraged you to take risks. Startups, particularly, but even ongoing, successful businesses require calculated risk. Libby provided the environment and culture to make that happen. It was okay to fail but even better to succeed. Oh, did we have fun!"

—**Mike Sick,** *former president, Connolly Healthcare and Cotiviti*

"I worked with Connolly and Associates for eight years. They were courteous, professional, and tenacious. During that time there were periods where I wouldn't see Libby Alexander for almost a year. She would be that pregnant lady working the trade shows and interacting with clients and potential clients. The next year, pregnant again and on the front lines. She charted her own course and was an inspiration to women that worked and had to raise a family at the same time. If I had this book back then, to see what was going on inside the company, I would have been even more astounded at her energy and drive!"

—**Nelda Barkley,** *founder and former CEO, IAPP*

"As a customer of Libby Connolly Alexander and her company, I had a wonderful opportunity to be part of an industry-wide transformation in the audit world. As the postaudit director of a major electronic retailer that was going through an explosion of electronic data, new innovative promotional strategies, acquisitions, and transformation into an omnichannel sales strategy, we needed a business partner who could help transform our ability to audit beyond what was historically called a box audit. Connolly brought us an audit model, a highly talented group of diverse-background auditors, and the capability to leverage state of the art technology, resulting in some incredibly innovative ways to identify and recover lost revenue, pricing, and promotional funds."

—**Grant Rabuse,** *former Best Buy director of postaudit*

"As I reflect on my twenty-one-year journey at Connolly, I cannot think of a more fitting title for this book than *Figuring It Out.* In my early years at Connolly, we were often the underdog, but we were scrappy! Larry and Libby recognized that we were all figuring it out, and wisely made personal and professional development a priority and an important part of our culture. At quarterly and annual leadership gatherings, there would always be time dedicated to professional development or training. We read a lot of books—some better than others—and heard from a lot of great speakers and authors. I never met Jim Connolly, but enjoyed learning more about his vision and values. They were embedded in the company's DNA, and for twenty-one years I witnessed the lasting effect they had on our successful approach to serving clients. *Figuring It Out* is a fascinating read for anyone interested in entrepreneurship, and will certainly capture the attention of anyone familiar with the recovery audit industry."

—**Anthony Massanelli,** *former president of global retail, Connolly, Inc. and Cotiviti*

"As one of Connolly's original principals, I first encountered paid bill auditing in 1957, and knew Jim Connolly since he came to Bloomingdale's. I have known Larry and Libby Connolly since they first joined their father in the '80s. Libby was sent to me for training, where minimizing client disruption and client consulting were emphasized. The industry today is nothing like what I knew in 1980s and 1990s. It is remarkable how Larry and Libby anticipated and adapted to these changes and pioneered a whole new business in healthcare, while remaking a loosely structured association between principals and auditors into a clearly defined and structured business. Theirs is a remarkable success story."

—**Bob Wessel,** *an original principal of Connolly Consulting Associates, Inc.*

"In late 2000, I took on the newly created role of vice president of vendor management for United Healthcare. On my first day, I received a phone call from my new supervisor telling me that my vendors were 'out of control' and that I specifically needed to fire Connolly. Having been in management for many years, I knew I had to form my own impressions.

"I reached out to Connolly and had some 'how are we going to figure this out' conversations with Mike Sick. This required my team and Connolly to develop much more of a 'trust' relationship, one that would result in each of us meeting our respective goals. It soon became apparent that Connolly was one of the few vendors who listened.

"As the results came in and quality improved, we continued to work on building an interface with Connolly, which included Larry and Libby and Rob Alexander from IT. Their involvement was integral to making this process successful, as we knew we had 'buy-in' from the top of the organization. Additionally, we knew we were dealing with a data and technology driven process, so Rob's participating proved the Connolly commitment.

"We gradually gained confidence. Over a period of years, we continued to grow our relationship with Connolly. I get great satisfaction that the one relationship I was supposed to terminate has been the one that has been maintained the longest. The business values Libby describes in *Figuring It Out* are what made this relationship lasting."

—**Bob Starman,** *vice president, business operations, Devlin Consulting Group; former vice president, audit and recovery operations, UnitedHealth Group*

FIGURING IT OUT

Best wishes to you
Along your journey of
figuring It Out

— _Ashley C. ____

1/20

LIBBY CONNOLLY ALEXANDER

FIGURING IT OUT

A MEMOIR ABOUT
CONNOLLY, INC'S
JOURNEY TO THE TOP

Published by Advantage, Charleston, South Carolina.
Member of Advantage Media Group.

ADVANTAGE is a registered trademark, and the Advantage colophon is a trademark of Advantage Media Group, Inc.

Printed in the United States of America.

10 9 8 7 6 5 4 3 2 1

ISBN: 978-1-64225-043-5
LCCN: 2019917127

Book design by Megan Elger.

This publication is designed to provide accurate and authoritative information in regard to the subject matter covered. It is sold with the understanding that the publisher is not engaged in rendering legal, accounting, or other professional services. If legal advice or other expert assistance is required, the services of a competent professional person should be sought.

Advantage Media Group is proud to be a part of the Tree Neutral® program. Tree Neutral offsets the number of trees consumed in the production and printing of this book by taking proactive steps such as planting trees in direct proportion to the number of trees used to print books. To learn more about Tree Neutral, please visit **www.treeneutral.com**.

Advantage Media Group is a publisher of business, self-improvement, and professional development books and online learning. We help entrepreneurs, business leaders, and professionals share their Stories, Passion, and Knowledge to help others Learn & Grow. Do you have a manuscript or book idea that you would like us to consider for publishing? Please visit **advantagefamily.com** or call **1.866.775.1696**.

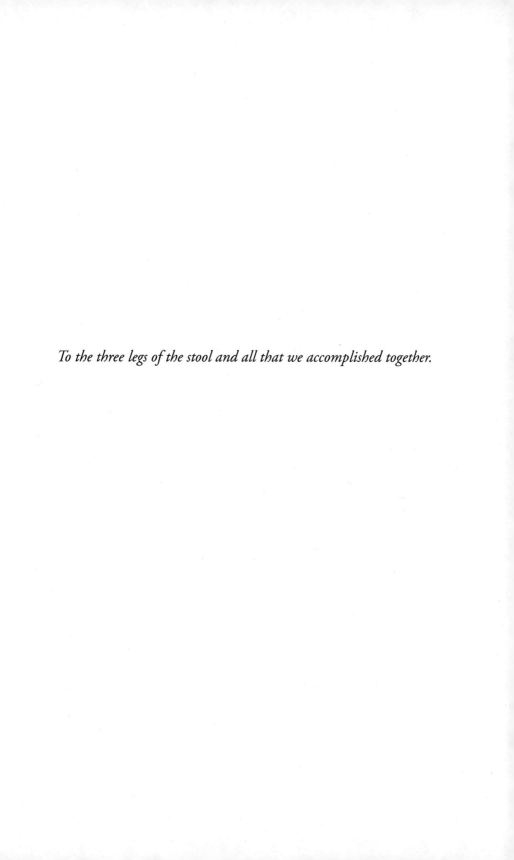

To the three legs of the stool and all that we accomplished together.

CONTENTS

ACKNOWLEDGMENTS

The idea for this book came from David Swift, Cotiviti's former executive chairman, in June of 2017. The company's board and several members of the management team were attending a baseball game at Atlanta's newly minted SunTrust Park. A retirement ceremony was scheduled before the first pitch for both my brother Larry and Mike Sick, my cousin and the former head of our healthcare group. Larry was retiring from the board and Mike was retiring from his post on the management team. I was asked and had the honor of speaking on behalf of both, acknowledging and bringing to the fore some of their many contributions to the company. After I was done, Dave approached me and asked something along the lines of, "Libby, you have a lot of great stories to tell. Have you ever considered writing a book?" That was the furthest thing from my mind at the time, but Dave's comment certainly got me thinking. Maybe it was the history major in me?

Shortly after, he provided some names and contacts who could help. I was intrigued but sat on the idea for a while until one random day I started to sort through the many boxes of documents I had accumulated in both my attic and basement. Some were from my former office at Cotiviti, some were from my personal memory box, and some were from our family house on Cape Cod. You see, when our family house was sold in 2012, we had a dilemma about what to do with some of my parents' personal stuff—old photos, business files from my father's office, and all the family memorabilia long stored in the Cape house attic. No one wanted to throw all that away, and no one was in a position to take it all home. Except me. Since I was the only one headed home in a car (my siblings lived far away at the time), my husband, Robert, threw my father's files, several boxes of memorabilia, and a trunk full of old photos into the back of our Suburban. Until I sat down with all that stuff one day, never did I imagine those family "treasures" would serve as the "trove" for a book not yet conceived. As I look back, I sincerely believe this project was meant for me. Thank you, Dave Swift, for planting the seed.

Kevin Clark—a.k.a. "Webster," as I affectionately call him, due to his attention to writing, correct spelling, and meticulous grammar—worked with me for over eighteen years. During that time, there wasn't a single presentation or speech, including my testimony before Congress in the summer of 2010, where he wasn't by my side helping me organize my thoughts or helping me find the right words when I struggled. The same is true of this project. My deepest thanks go to Kevin for agreeing to work with me again. I wouldn't have been able to write the memoir without him. He knows and loves the Connolly story, he knows my "voice," and sometimes he knows what I want to communicate even better than I do. Neither of us had ever written a book before, but together, we figured it out.

In preparation for the book, I interviewed many Connolly colleagues and friends of the firm who helped me understand what made Connolly *Connolly* to them. They also helped me sharpen my recollection of the events that marked our collective journey, and what made that journey most noteworthy. Thank you to everyone I spoke, met, or corresponded with, especially Tony Massanelli, Ryan Mooney, Mike Matloub, Herb Baron, Jeff Thomas, and Tom Santacroce. Tom also gave me the idea of using a photo of the Clocktower on the cover.

A highlight of working on this was the afternoon I spent with Bob Wessel last January. At ninety-one years of age, Bob insisted on driving to my home in Rye, where we spent a day together in front of a warm fire reminiscing about the retail landscape in the '60s-'80s, how he met my father, his career at Connolly, and my time working for him at Montgomery Ward in Chicago in the early '90s. That day, January 11, 2019, is a day I will always cherish.

Both Mike Sick and Peter Campisi were instrumental in helping me reconstruct our foray into healthcare. Without these two Connolly pioneers, there would be less to write about, and my career would not have been as noteworthy nor as fun.

Upon completion of my final draft, I reached out to several colleagues and former clients who read the manuscript and provided feedback under very tight timelines. I am grateful for your time and the testimonials you provided. Most importantly, I appreciate your being part of the project!

Jim Riehl was a second and third set of eyes, who gave the final manuscript a critical and objective sanity check. His meticulous chapter by chapter notes and feedback helped us rework and fine tune various aspects of the storyline that we didn't get quite right the first time around. He also lent his creativity, and it was Jim's idea to add the dimension of a timeline to the beginning of each chapter.

To the team at my publisher, Advantage, especially Tiara Butler, thank you for all the hand holding and support. Tiara, your sensitivity is noteworthy. There were many aspects of this project that were delicate, requiring extra steps you were always willing to take to make things right. You are also a graceful coach, and got me through the most emotional aspects of the memoir that I found difficult to write. For a publisher to engage with a first-time author, especially one who has perfectionist tendencies and is as green as I am, means lots of extra work. The team was always very patient and supportive. I learned a ton, especially about overshooting word counts! All I can say is that the extra 21,000-plus words were necessary. I could have used some more, but "guard rails" are good, too.

A career such as mine would not have been manageable if it were not for the stability I had at home during my career years at Connolly. For more than twenty years, Brenda Bagley faithfully and lovingly helped me and Robert raise our four children, who are only five years apart in age from first to fourth. Our work life required constant travel and long days at the office. Brenda was our capable backbone at home. She is a special person, whom we love, along with her son, Reed, very much.

My capacity as an effective executive was multiplied with the support I received from my administrative assistants, especially Margerie Sibiski and Laura Asquino. These gals were organizational powerhouses who orchestrated the daily schedule and so much more. They were intimately woven into both my professional and personal life, and simply made everything better. Our good days were good days together. So were the bad. We shared more than a few laughs, and a few tears along the way, too. For those who wondered how I managed it all, well, now you know. These two and Brenda. Life was better with the three of you!

My Dunning Road neighbor, running pal, therapist, and true friend, Sally Campbell, was and continues to be always there for me—rain or shine, sleet or snow, mornings that were both dark and light, but always at dawn. Sally is a remarkable person, admirable mother, and the best neighbor ever. Thank you for all the life advice and especially for getting me through the toughest moments of my DCIS treatments.

At the outset, my two oldest siblings, Jimmy Connolly and Carol Connolly, provided their personal reflections of our dad as both a father and a businessman. Their accounts were invaluable, helping me pinpoint his traits and piece together the narrative pre-Libby. Both also provided me the encouragement I needed to take this project on and to see it through to the end. The two of them have been lifelong cheerleaders to their baby sister, and a constant source of love and support. Sadly, and unexpectedly, our family lost Jimmy in November 2018. Jim was a literary genius and had tremendous command over the English language, and so I was dreading his critique of this book. Now I would accept it gladly if it meant still having him in my life. I will forever love him and miss him.

I am most grateful to my husband, Robert, and my family. They have always given me unwavering support and the space I needed to prioritize this all-consuming "retirement" project over the past year and a half. I am truly blessed and love you all beyond words.

Finally, I would like to express my gratitude to Larry for giving so generously of his time. He graciously participated in multiple telephone interviews, filling in gaps and providing perspective. He also spent invaluable time "auditing" the manuscript and provided invaluable feedback. For anyone reading this memoir who knows us or who worked with us, please understand that I wrote it to memorialize the story behind the business as I perceived it, but also, and perhaps more importantly, to share my personal journey at Connolly. The focus of the book is naturally more about me, my perspectives, and my experiences over the course of my thirty-year career working for the firm. It is fair to say Larry's memoir would read differently. Naturally, our individual experiences and recollections, as well as the importance each of us assigns to certain milestones and events, differ significantly. Despite those differences, Larry and I agree on many of the things we accomplished together under his leadership as president and then CEO from 1990–2012, a period where Connolly saw astonishing growth. I love you, Larry, and I thank you from the bottom of my heart.

Connolly, Inc.
COMPANY TIMELINE

James Aloysius Connolly is born in Scranton, PA

1979
Larry Connolly joins JACA, assisting on audit work

1980

CCA revenue surpasses $1 mil

1984

1921

1979

1982

James Connolly, CEO and Founder, starts Recovery Audit firm James A. Connolly & Associates (JACA)

JACA changes its name to "Connolly Consulting Associates" (CCA)

Libby Connolly joins CCA as Administrative Assistant

CCA reaches $5 mil in sales

1990
Robert Alexander divests Alexander Systems and joins CCA

1996

CCA establishes Commercial Recovery Audit Division

1997

1989

1993

1996

CCA names Larry Connolly COO and Libby Connolly Alexander Exec VP of Administration

CCA ownership transfers from James Connolly to Larry Connolly and Libby Connolly Alexander

CCA establishes United Kingdom Recovery Audit Division

CCA enters Healthcare Recovery Audit market

1998
Connolly converts from Independent Contractor to Employee organization

2001

CCA achieves more than $50 mil in sales

2005

1998

2001

2004

James A. Connolly, Founder, passes

Connolly adds second and third healthcare clients

CCA rebrands itself as simply "Connolly"

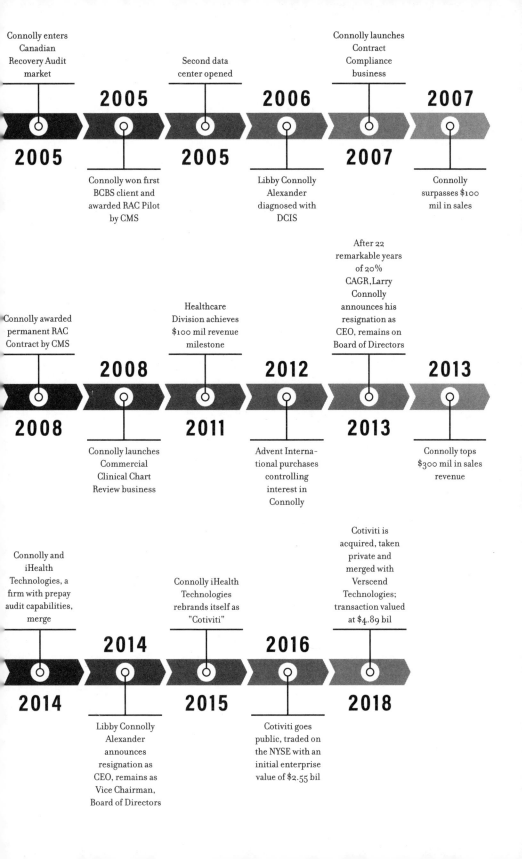

INTRODUCTION

The Rise of Connolly, Inc.

If you're going to do something, do it right—or don't do it at all.

—A Jim Connolly mantra

A
fter years of following the traditional American dream, forging a path that allowed him to rise through the ranks of the retail world, my father came home one day with an announcement that would change the future of our family for generations. While we were gathered for dinner, he announced to us he would be leaving his position as the chief operating officer of Gimbels department store in New York City. No longer would he be leading one of the country's largest and most respected department stores. The comfort and security of his corporate accomplishments

would be left behind to follow a dream of a different sort. With eyes void of doubt, my father shared his plans to embark on a new venture, one that none of us entirely understood.

I was still in high school at the time, and the inexperience of my youth prevented me from fully comprehending what courage it must have taken, the way he must have felt, the day he made this important decision. As a relatively old executive at fifty-eight years of age, my father was stepping out into the unknown of entrepreneurship, a move virtually unheard of for a man of his generation. The risk was taken during a time when the demand for financial stability in our family was high. My father had put his two oldest through college already, had one finishing, and had another—me—on the way to undergrad. This had left him with two substantial mortgages on our house, not to mention the demands of maintaining the upper-middle-class lifestyle he'd created as a well-paid retail executive. If there was ever a right time to start a business, most would agree this was not it.

Many men of his generation would have cringed at the thought of self-employment and opted for the comfort and security of the corporate world instead. They would have sought out another position to give them the confidence that comes from bringing home a paycheck to support their families. Most would never have sacrificed the daily rides on the commuter train, which was a time for fellowship with a well-dressed who's who of almost every industry. Those trips to the city were compounded with a number of executive perks—cushy corner offices, secretaries to bring coffee, catered lunches, luxury clubs, exclusive parties, and all the other trappings most men used to measure their success during this time. Fully aware his decision posed a fair amount of risk, my father chose a different path, one that would immerse my entire family in a nascent business filled with uncertainty.

That decision is what inspired me to write this book. After nearly thirty years of operating a thriving recovery auditing business that expanded well beyond the confines of what anyone else could have ever dreamed up, I sit here reflecting on how far we've come. We owe everything to my father's decision to take a risk. All the success the Connolly business—and in turn the Connolly and Alexander families—realized can be traced back to one man's brave decision. My father gave us a blueprint masterfully explaining the core values and principles that support any successful business, a blueprint I've mapped out in this book.

In the pages to come, I plan to carry you on a journey charting the growth and expansion of my family and our business through four decades of hard work and commitment. They keys to success passed down to me and my brother helped us forge the way for a professional adventure none of us ever anticipated. I plan to hand those same keys over to you in this book. My father's example became the foundation for our every business move. It showed us to never fear being first and to always remember why you took that first step. As the first in his family to attend college, he was not a stranger to hard work. Scraping together the funds to finance his dream was just the beginning of many challenges he'd be forced to face over the years.

Having served as a naval officer in the South Pacific during World War II, he'd acquired many lifelong skills while in his prime. Not only did the military teach him to be fearless, selfless, and willing to take calculated risks for the betterment of all, it was his wartime pay

My father gave us a blueprint masterfully explaining the core values and principles that support any successful business, a blueprint I've mapped out in this book.

that helped him earn an MBA from Harvard University, a decision that helped jump-start the future of his professional career. Today, I assume the task of telling his story—our story—in hopes that our work will inspire generations to come.

Married with four children to support, why would a successful finance executive part ways with the legacy he'd established at various retailers to traipse into the unknown?

Upon the discovery of a number of letters, documents, and commentary exchanged through our family and business over the years, I believe I have pieced together a few answers to this question and others. Within those answers, I seem to have unveiled a valuable message with the power to instruct and inspire anyone who may be straddling the fence, anyone who may be curious about the type of future they can create for themselves.

As one of two offspring who took over this remarkable business germinated from my father's dreams, I've learned leading change takes courage. Working alongside my brother Larry, I quickly learned that, to become Connolly's future CEOs, we would have to open ourselves to be pushed further than we would have ever known. We would need to learn to listen and to be self-sacrificial. We would learn how much one can create when you allow a little competitive paranoia to serve as your motivation. We would have to *change*, which is a lesson in itself.

> *To become Connolly's future CEOs, we would have to open ourselves to be pushed further than we would have ever known.*

Before our business was born, we watched our father fall victim to the winds of change buffeting the retail world in the late 1970s: the conglomerates, junk bonds, and management shake-ups that left many dazed and uncertain. His propensity to figure it out while scaling his way through a business that at the time was largely unproven created the opportunity for my brother, my husband, and me to contribute our raw expertise to help build what ultimately became a nearly $5 billion business.

If you are familiar with what Connolly, Inc.—or Cotiviti, as it's named today—has become, you'd be amazed to learn the multibillion-dollar company was started in a spare bedroom of our home in Rye, New York.

In the beginning, every part of our business was built through modest, personal investments. Never out to grow into more than he could manage, my father weighed his options and played the hand he was dealt. Self-financed and arranged with nothing more than his firsthand understanding of the industry, the business James A. Connolly built was nothing short of amazing. This was not a case of creating something in an industry that was already well established. In every sense of the word, he built the business—and in turn helped create the industry it was a part of—from the ground up.

Before I descend into the adventure that became my life as a mother and a businesswoman, I want to start by introducing you to the man behind the vision. I want to offer you a glimpse into my father, the man and the professional.

As a visual aid, I have decided to share some of my historical finds with you. Follow along with the company's timeline at the start of the book as I walk you through our evolution in each chapter. This book details the calculated risks required for us to build Connolly into what it became. It tells of finding a path forward and learning at every turn.

I share with you all the things required of us to transform, build, and expand the business from a modest mom-and-pop business into a globally recognized brand. Our unconventional approach yielded a few unconventional revelations along the way. In hindsight, I discovered that, while technology was a catalyst for our company's success, perhaps our best assets were our *people*. Investments into talented minds who shared our passion and entrepreneurial style allowed us the pleasure of having people like my husband, Robert, and so many other smart and dedicated associates by our side. As we grew, Connolly adopted the idea that even if something had not been done by anyone before, that did not mean that it could not be done by us.

As I always shared with the teams I led, my goal for Connolly was never to be the biggest; I only wanted us to be the best. I invested over thirty years of my life toward achieving that goal, and now that I've finally relinquished my executive responsibilities, I feel the story of this family's journey is worth chronicling for posterity. Within these pages, you'll find many of the valuable business lessons professionals seek from books of this kind. Still, amid the takeaways from the many decisions we had to make over the years—most of which were decided on the spot—you'll also discover the story of many people who helped us achieve the remarkable success created by our little homegrown family business.

You'll learn of our victories and learn from our mistakes.

While this book is certainly a family tale, it is also very much the story of how the greatest success comes from having a team willing to move like a well-oiled machine. Let these chapters serve as my thank-you to those who invested themselves into Connolly's success, treating our business as if it were their own. Let it stand as a time capsule containing evidence of the way one dedicated group was willing to figure it out regardless of the risks, a guideline that governs all the different nuances contributing to this rewarding voyage of accomplishment.

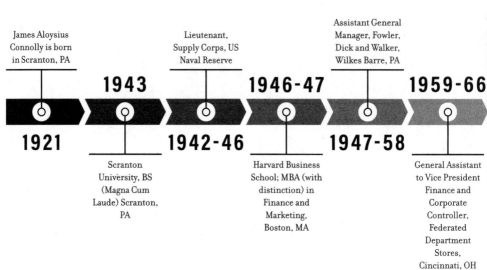

James Aloysius
Connolly is born
in Scranton, PA

1943

Lieutenant,
Supply Corps, US
Naval Reserve

1946-47

Assistant General
Manager, Fowler,
Dick and Walker,
Wilkes Barre, PA

1959-66

1921

1942-46

1947-58

Scranton
University, BS
(Magna Cum
Laude) Scranton,
PA

Harvard Business
School; MBA (with
distinction) in
Finance and
Marketing,
Boston, MA

General Assistant
to Vice President
Finance and
Corporate
Controller,
Federated
Department
Stores,
Cincinnati, OH

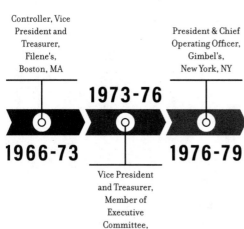

Controller, Vice
President and
Treasurer,
Filene's,
Boston, MA

1973-76

President & Chief
Operating Officer,
Gimbel's,
New York, NY

1966-73

1976-79

Vice President
and Treasurer,
Member of
Executive
Committee,
Bloomingdale's,
New York, NY

CHAPTER 1

My Father's Footsteps

The Groundwork for Success

Above all, learn and constantly practice the art of adjusting to change.

—James A. Connolly

Among the many treasures I've collected over the years is a letter my father wrote to all his children in recognition of his seventy-fifth birthday. He had invited the family to celebrate his milestone birthday at our family's house on Cape Cod. He loved the Cape house, with its magnificent waterfront views and deep-water dock. Of course, you cannot forget to mention his prized boat, *Duet*, and the tall flagpole in the yard with its patriotic flag gloriously waving in the wind. We gathered at the house many times over the years, but there was something special about this day.

Picture children running around in bathing suits, laughing and playing. Pony rides keeping them entertained whenever they could pull themselves away from the sweet, juicy watermelon laid out on a picnic table. The mouthwatering aroma of food on the grill. The sun shining down on us with its approving glow. There was this feeling in the air, something indescribable. Thinking about the smiles plastered on everyone's faces, I guess I would say that the moment felt like *love*.

The glorious day was my father's birthday, but for all who were there, it was a celebration to remember. We served cake. Children, relatives, and friends gave toasts and made speeches about how much my father meant to them. When dusk arrived, we closed the evening by firing off Calamity Jane, my father's prized cannon, to commemorate the event. Then, when it was all said and done, we lowered the flags, and the children shuffled off to bed. Everyone had a wonderful time, but the nature of the party caused us to overlook one very important detail.

With so much happening, our dedications had interfered with my father's plan to deliver one of his coveted speeches. If anyone knew Jim Connolly, they knew how much he loved to share a good, heartfelt sentiment. At the time, no one realized how badly he wanted to grace us with his prepared thoughts, but he most certainly never forgot.

After the festivities, he sat down at his computer and typed a few good words to his children.

```
I am aware of my reputation (largely unde-
served, in my view) for occasionally being
long winded. And surely, when you consider
```

the goodly number of major venues in which I have lived (three separate ones in my boyhood in Scranton alone; Allentown, in the Navy; Notre Dame, New England, Washington, DC, the Chesapeake, California, the far reaches of the South and Central Pacific, including New Zealand; Harvard, Wyoming Valley, Cincinnati, Wellesley, and Boston; Rye and New York City; Florida and Cape Cod) and all the wonderful places we've visited on DUET — plus the epochs through which I've been blessed to live (the Depression, World War II, Korea, Vietnam, and more than forty years of the Cold War) … well, I ought to be able to put together on my seventy-fifth birthday something worth saying. And I am sorely tempted to punish my critics in my family by laying out for them the full nine yards of my completely unabridged autobiography!

You've all heard it said, "The only thing certain in life is death and taxes."

Well, death is merely the change of one form of being for another, and taxes is merely a change in who spends the money you earn, you or the government.

So, in reality, the only thing certain in

```
life is change.
```

```
And the single most important lesson I've
learned from the wonderful assortment of
life experiences that have been mine thus
far is that one enjoys and prospers in life
in direct proportion to how much he excels
in the art of adjusting to change.
```

It is easy to understand why change was such an important concept to my father. Change became a recurring theme throughout his life and career. He made the conscious decision to change everything he'd grown accustomed to as a retail executive to venture off and start his own recovery audit business, Connolly Consulting Associates (CCA). If he only knew then what that company would grow to be.

LEARN TO ADAPT TO YOUR ENVIRONMENT

While I was piecing together this story, what became clear was that many of my father's decisions were propelled by his willingness to listen to his gut. He did so in a way that was never impulsive but instead respectful of the direction chance and circumstance can take you, if you do your part.

Change calls for you to adapt to your environment and learn to feel your way through the unknown. Do not be mistaken: change *will* happen, usually when you least expect it. Whenever it does, the way you respond to that change determines so much about the future you will create for yourself.

My father's humble upbringing did not allude to the life he would one day lead. My grandmother passed away at the age of fifty-one when my father was just twenty-five, and my grandfather soon followed her at age sixty-one. You can see why that seventy-fifth birthday was such a momentous occasion for my family.

Unlike many of his peers, my father could not rely on his parents' wisdom and guidance. This created a new set of challenges, especially during some of the most pivotal times of his life.

Before they passed, my grandparents built a modest life in Scranton, Pennsylvania. Back then the Coal Capital, known for its rich locomotive history, was a little more populous than it is today, probably because most people never left! It was one of those areas where you lived with whatever life offered you and did not ask questions. For some reason, my father chose to look beyond the limits many of his neighbors accepted.

He was not a stranger to embracing change and doing whatever it took to stay on top of his dreams. Rather than play the hand he was dealt, he developed a "figure it out" mentality.

I do believe he always planned to succeed, but I don't think he anticipated Connolly growing to where it earned business from nearly all of the top twenty retailers in the country, and I know he never imagined the day we'd have a roster of healthcare clients like Aetna, Humana, and UnitedHealthcare, with multimillion-dollar accounts to manage. My father's vision, though consistent and firm, never called for praise and recognition. The way he moved, the way he managed the business, the way he raised his children, all of this derived from the values he developed in his youth.

As a teen, he worked to become the first of his family to go to college, attending Scranton University. Before our company

Jim Connolly was on a mission to do nothing more than wake up as a better version of the man he was the day before.

ever sparked a fire inside his mind, Jim Connolly was on a mission to do nothing more than wake up as a better version of the man he was the day before.

You would think someone with so much conviction would eventually become a bit bigheaded and self-serving, but amazingly enough, my father never became that man. He moved with integrity and humility, always working toward benefiting the collective.

My dad did what he felt was right. I saw it as I shadowed him through life, but the picture really came into focus when I read over some of his old journals from the military.

I learned that my father, Lieutenant James Aloysius Connolly, was honorably discharged from the US Navy after three years, nine months, and two days of duty. Because of his commitment, he was awarded various ribbons for his service. After reading through his journals, I realized how those decorations reflected the way he selflessly committed himself to his fellow man.

In that stack of records, there was a letter he wrote while reflecting on his time as a naval officer. It struck me as a prime example of how he exercised his values, even in the most strenuous situations.

He was in his early twenties at the time, serving on the deck of the SS *Platano*. Thrust into an unfamiliar environment, he was forced to navigate through the strained climate caused by the war and the socioeconomic struggles suffocating the world. In the photo gallery at the back of the book, you probably noticed a photo of him standing aboard the ship overlooking the Leyte Gulf, where the renowned General MacArthur was to make his famous return to the Philippines. What an amazing piece of history!

The *Platano* was a Central American banana ship recommissioned as a supply ship of the US Navy auxiliary during the Second World War. To man ships like the *Platano*, the navy sent promising college-educated enlistees like my father through an eight-week crash course in officer training at schools such as Notre Dame. From there, many were shipped off to Harvard Business School, where they spent twenty weeks learning what it took to be logistics supply officers. Upon completion, the men were cleared to sail to the South Pacific to offer some assistance. This letter sets the stage for the challenges awaiting my father at sea:

> My ship, the SS *Platano*, was assigned to provision ships in Amphibious Group 12, composed of roughly fifty-five attack personnel and cargo ships, 150 landing craft of various types, twenty-four destroyers, and fifty miscellaneous small ships that were staging in Leyte Gulf, P.I., in March 1945, in preparations for landing the Seventh and Seventy-Seventh Army Divisions on Okinawa.

Originally commissioned to carry banana cargo from Central America to the East Coast, his ship was already about fifteen years old. Apparently, it was not properly outfitted for military service, but my father and his fellow shipmen were expected to make the most of their resources.

The voyage to the South Pacific was not an easy trip. The ships did not have proper temperature controls, and the tropical climate made it difficult to preserve fresh cargo. The soldiers had already taken the initiative to fabricate a makeshift intership phone system themselves, but there was little that could be done to get around the inevitable: high temperatures meant the food was going to spoil long before they reached the Philippines. At least, that was how most people viewed the situation. Lieutenant Connolly, on the other hand, chose a different perspective.

Even in his prime, my father never settled for defeat. He was given a task, and he took it to heart. Surveying quite frankly the conditions the men were forced to endure at sea, he found it unacceptable. As I read his letter, I got a glimpse into how he planned to fix the situation.

> If working parties didn't bring their own chow, they had to be returned to their own ships to be fed. My responsibility included the physical movement of provisions to the receiving ships as well as accounting for their disposal. My department consisted of seven-rated storekeepers, all good men, and we were solely responsible for cargo operations aboard the *Platano*.

> When the *Platano* put in to Hollandia, en route from Auckland to Leyte, I decided to issue to ships to present the entire cargo of lettuce and celery while it was still in good condition, rather than risk spoilage before arrival destination.

He figured it out. Without an established process for delivering the food to hungry seamen, my father decided that he would have to come up with one. He issued—delivered—his cargo of food to the ships present rather than wait. Some might have argued that he would have been justified if he simply waited around for a superior to provide direction, watching the food rot in the heat. Instead, he chose to take the lead.

These men needed food.

Their food was spoiling.

Time was of the essence.

Thanks to his decision to take initiative, thousands of men were fed. His superiors recognized what he had done and extended their blessing, but after the fact. Boarding the ship, he was nothing more than a hopeful barely twentysomething, and with his very first assignment, he earned the respect of his peers and was regarded as a leader among the men.

Finally, the *Platano* arrived in the Leyte Gulf on March 17, 1945.[1] It was my father's first visit to the Philippines, and I do not think any amount of training could have prepared him for what was to come. He details some of the chaos as his letter continues:

[We were met] passing through the harbor nets by representatives from eight transports desiring food immediately. Since this was our first visit to Leyte, we did not know who the cognizant service squadron commander was or where he could be located among the several hundred ships present. The officers wishing to draw rations had no specific orders to do so, nor could they help me learn where I might go for our orders.

When we anchored at 2000 and no service squadron representative had yet reported aboard, I decided to issue to these ships.

It was a calculated risk that paid off tremendously. He had assessed the situation and taken action rather than aimlessly waiting

---

1   James A. Connolly, naval service sketch.

around for directions. His superiors did not show up until much later in the evening; those men would have gone mad if they were forced to wait for food that was in sight. To the ranking members' surprise, the *Platano* had completed its operation earlier than anticipated. All rations were dispersed, and everyone received a fair portion.

Lieutenant Connolly did not have a lot of time to learn and adjust to what was expected of him. The decisions he made were based on the inherent values that made up his character. This letter took me on a detailed journey into my father's mind. It painted a picture that proved being young and inexperienced did not mean one could not deliver well above what was expected.

Bringing things into focus, there was another monumental moment that took place during this time. Leyte Gulf was the scene of World War II's largest naval battle. This event was forever engraved in history as the first time the Japanese deployed kamikazes—suicide planes—as a weapon. Many years later, the tactic of a kamikaze attack was something my father would reference during a pivotal moment in his career. More on that later.

INVESTING FOR THE FUTURE

Try to imagine the state of the country as we battled through World War II. When the time for peace was called, the navy ordered all its seamen home. Arriving stateside, my father had only $3,000 left from his military salary. In 1947, he used a good portion of that savings to return to Harvard Business School to study accounting. Earning his MBA with distinction (he graduated third in his class) was yet another way he was embracing change. America was still attempting to recover from the war, and opportunities were scarce. This time, Jim Connolly decided to take a calculated risk on himself.

The decision to advance into entrepreneurship did not happen overnight. After graduating from Harvard, he went back to Pennsylvania and accepted a job offer from Frank Burnside, the owner of a family-run department store in Wilkes-Barre called Fowler, Dick & Walker. With only a single location, the business ran an impressive $8 million operation. My father was hired on as the assistant general manager with a starting annual salary of only $3,600. For ten years, he worked alongside Frank, building a relationship that served my family in more ways than one.[2]

During that time, my father started to experience change of a more intimate nature. He courted a Wilkes-Barre girl, Connie Green, my mother, and they married in 1950. Within three years, a son, James Aloysius Connolly III, was born, and they were expecting their second child. The relationship my father developed with the owner of Fowler, Dick & Walker eventually created the opportunity for him to purchase his first house. One of the benefits of buying your boss's home is, if you're lucky, he will sell it to you for an incredible discount.

Even with the reduced asking price, my father required a bit of assistance to help cover the down payment. Frank did not hesitate to give him a loan. Everyone has heard sayings like, "It pays to be a good person." Well, in this case, truer words could not have been spoken.

Jim Connolly invested everything he had into expanding the operations at Fowler, Dick & Walker. After a decade of commitment, he started to realize there was something missing from his job. In a random revelation, he concluded that, regardless of how much he deposited into that business, there was only so far for him to advance.

You see, Frank had a son who would one day inherit the entire

---

2   James A. Connolly, "Professional and Financial Background." Prudential Securities (PSI) arbitration.

company. Fowler, Dick & Walker could reap the benefits of my father's commitment, but he would never be able to claim it as his own.

Aside from that, the economy in Wilkes-Barre was struggling. Not only that, but limited opportunity placed the town's potential at a standstill. Eventually, my father started to feel the weight of being restricted to a subordinate position in the business:

> At F.D. & W., for all my effort and service, I still was not felt qualified to gaze upon the financial statements — much too private.

I wonder if it hurt him to know that he had invested so much into helping this business grow, only to learn that they still did not find him "worthy" of reviewing their financial reports. That truth may never be revealed, but living in honor of his values prompted my father to make another major decision.

In 1959, change reared its cunning head yet again, this time in the form of an offer to continue his retail career as an assistant corporate controller at Federated Department Stores, a massive operation that was steadily growing by the day. Just consider Federated as the Amazon of its time.

Living in honor of his values prompted my father to make another major decision.

Taking the position at Federated, a much larger operation than what he managed in Wilkes-Barre, was a big deal to my father and his young family—not only because my father was about to take a promotion, but also because this position required him to move to Cincinnati, Ohio.

This promotion began as a calculated risk, one my mother was not very happy about at first. I have stacks of letters exchanged between them during his transition while he was in Cincinnati and my mother was still in Wilkes-Barre trying to sell their house so they could buy a new one. She wanted her husband around, and he just wanted her to trust and believe in him.

In my father's defense, he did not leave her out in the cold. My father knew that, in Pennsylvania, my mother had the support of her parents and five siblings. Even with children to take care of, he trusted in her family's willingness to help while he was gone.

He knew they would be around. Families stayed together, especially when the war became infamous for tearing families apart. It wasn't common for people in towns like Wilkes-Barre to leave, especially while leaving their wives and children behind. Moving away and starting over was something people just did not do during those times. More often, modest opportunities that presented themselves on a local level were pursued. Being married to Jim Connolly meant you had to change your world view. He saw things differently, so my mother was required to expect the unexpected and believe in his vision. Despite the way things may have seemed from the outside looking in, my father was following his intuition. It was a calculated risk that would start laying the building blocks for the future of his legacy.

While they were writing each other back and forth, my father swore my mother to secrecy about the reasons behind their plans. He didn't want to burn bridges, nor be judged for taking such a risky step. The last thing he wanted was for him and my mother to be scrutinized for his decision.

People were very image conscious back then. Well, not much has changed today. Still, they were living in a time when you measured a person's worth by the position they held, the clothes they wore, and the circles they entertained. Moving to Cincinnati was a step outside of their comfort zone. It was foreign. An unknown place.

My father decided it was a risk worth taking, so he let his ambition serve as a compass to guide him toward new opportunity.

FAITH IN CHANGE

I dove deeper into these letters, sending myself on a nostalgic trip through time. I gained an even greater understanding of what my parents were up against while my father was in Cincinnati. At first, my mother struggled to accept my father's plan, but her fears were put to rest by the confidence she had in her husband.

As I read his words and digested how much he believed in his decision, my eyes opened to the possibilities he saw. I almost felt as if he was sharing his story directly with me, all these years later.

In one of the letters from 1959, he quotes his wife as she gave him her blessing. She said, "I am willing and happy to do whatever you think is best."

And he writes:

You fully understood a change would mean great changes in your life, and that of your children, And in spite of the fact that you fully understood that there would be little or no control you personally could exercise over events once they had been started in motion, that was your answer of utter and complete devotion and confidence in me. And I shall never forget you in that moment.

Despite the challenges it placed on their personal relationship, there was an upside to taking the risk of moving and changing careers. His salary rose to $15,000, and his circle shifted to include some well-established gentlemen in the retail industry. Working for Federated soon became the second leg of what evolved into an outstanding professional career.

When I think back on his vision and determination, I'm not sure if he even fully appreciated all his best qualities. If he had not taken the risk to move to Cincinnati, he would have never been in the position to make the many connections that would later resurface as assets to Connolly.

Of all the men he collaborated with during his tenure at Federated, one man stands out from the crowd. Sam Parks, the "traveling Federated auditor" out of St. Louis, Missouri, befriended my father during my parents' separation in the spring and summer

> *If he had not taken the risk to move to Cincinnati, he would have never been in the position to make the many connections that would later resurface as assets to Connolly.*

of 1959. Sam was performing an internal audit for the company, and my father was working toward his next promotion as the general assistant to the vice president of finance. Sam was freshly assigned to conduct an examination at Shilito, and for my father, being new in town, it seemed natural that the two hit it off. Sam's assignment was scheduled to last for the next few months, and my father was still trying to get established in Cincinnati, so the two men decided it made sense to rent an apartment together.

Now roommates, they found ways to spend their leisure time together. They would go out for drinks and shoot pool, watch a baseball game, or visit a museum. Whenever they weren't at work, they were hanging out together, enjoying each other's company. My father got a taste of life on the whim, and Sam got to benefit from their many intellectual exchanges. It is those types of relationships that helped Connolly thrive when my father decided to start the business nearly twenty years later.

80 PERCENT IS NEVER ENOUGH

There was no sliding scale with Jim Connolly. Either you hit your mark, or you did not. When he put his efforts into completing a task, 80 percent was never good enough. He expected 100 percent effort; nothing else was acceptable.

No matter what he was involved in, my father set out to extract as much value from the experience as he could. He pushed himself to get better and improve, even when he did not have to. That is what made him such an incredible businessman and a groundbreaking entrepreneur.

Moving to Cincinnati called for some heavy consideration. Jim Connolly was not someone who took a risk for risk's sake. His plans were always calculated. He was very strategic.

In fact, he spent the duration of his thirty-two years in retail building a career that would continue to serve him long after the positions faded away. He spent nearly half of that time personally presiding over numerous major electronic data-processing system implementations, designing more efficient operations, and leading challenging conversion projects for his employers.

When he was in retail, my father had to respond to a new era of automation. An experiential learning strategy helped him thrive in the face of such drastic industry changes. He helped prominent retailers overhaul all their major systems, including POS, sales distribution, separate stocks and gross margin accounting, planning and reporting, fashion unit control, credit and collection, payroll and expense accounting, budgeting, and more. Change was all around him, and he rose to the occasion.

In only a short amount of time, change started to consume his existence. What began as him testing the waters to guarantee this was the best decision for our family quickly evolved into a change in his home, his job title, his responsibilities, and, even better, his salary. Now that was a welcome bonus!

Let's pause for a moment to consider the state of business in America circa the mid-1900s.

These were the years following the Great Depression of the 1930s and the Second World War. One should be able to gather a lot from that statement alone. Our country was struggling to revive a suffocated economic environment, and retailers were trying to think outside of the box to boost their sales in a new consumer-driven economy. They needed men like my father to help them crunch hard numbers and figure out a way to make their merchandise more accessible. Hence the emergence of things like store credit, designed to get consumers shopping again.

That also paved the way for retailers to get tangled in a brand-new set of issues. New payment-processing systems created new errors on the front and back end. The slightest variant in a purchase order could mean the difference in thousands of dollars' worth of revenue for a single store.

Federated was gobbling up retail real estate during this time. The company brokered a few lucrative mergers and acquisitions that really solidified its position in the market. It joined forces with so many powerful names that its steady expansion was all but guaranteed for the next few decades. Frequently receiving praise and acknowledgment from his peers, my father's performance proved he had a certain je ne sais quoi that separated him from the average executive. With the company's growth, that meant he would soon become the benefactor of a few well-placed promotions.

His tenure with Federated took a considerable leap when he was promoted to controller of Filene's, Boston, in mid-1966. Once he was there, he directed the development of several major systems, namely a few comprehensive and advanced payables systems, like the POM system, which was later installed and implemented at several other Federated department store locations.

My father was making an impact, and his efforts did not go unnoticed. Before long, his reputation and outstanding performance earned him the position of chief financial officer and treasury vice president and a $50,000 annual salary. A few years later, he was transferred to Bloomingdale's, another Federated division and its crown jewel, to hold the same position but with a $40,000 salary increase, a promising wage for a man in that era.

My father held that position from 1973 to 1976. I was pleased to come across a glimpse into the climate of the times after reading *Like No Other Store*, the memoir of Marvin Traub, the Bloomingdale's marketing legend. In his words, "The seventies were the decade when Bloomingdale's came into its own."

The work they were doing within the company was being recognized near and far. In fact, on December 1, 1975, Bloomingdale's made the cover of *Time* magazine in its headline description, "U.S. Shopping Surge, Trendy Bloomingdale's." Even the queen of England came to pay a visit to the retail mogul in July 1976, just before my father left to join Gimbels in August.

With so many retail-world changes and my father's executive achievements, what was even more impressive to me was his discipline to defer a good percentage of his salary for many years. In doing so, he was preparing himself to eventually finance his own business.

THE KAMIKAZE MISSION

In mid-1976, I took what I knew was a kamikaze assignment as president of Gimbels New York, but I had a plan for my own business and felt that if I could persevere to the completion of my contract, I would have gained the wherewithal to finance that transition. My salary was $145,000 annually, of which I deferred about $100,000 over the next three years (at a meager 5.5 percent interest). My contract was not renewed at its expiration December 31, 1979 — a situation I had been aware of and thusly had been able to prepare for over the preceding six to seven months.[3]

After working at Bloomingdale's for a short while, my father had taken on a suicide mission of sorts, one he dubbed "the kamikaze mission," undoubtedly inspired by what he experienced while in the Leyte Gulf during the war.

His next assignment was designed to be brief, and, ultimately, he knew he was working himself out of a position (hence the suicide reference). But he had a plan. As the president of Gimbels New York, owned by the Brown & Williamson tobacco company, with eleven stores and $200 million in sales, his new salary would afford him enough money to comfortably launch his own business.

Gimbels operated divisions in New York City, Philadelphia, Pittsburgh, and Milwaukee. Just think about that for a moment: a tobacco company moving into the retail sector. It was becoming a recurring theme in corporate America: conglomerates were buying a bunch of businesses outside their core operations. Businesses they knew very little about, to be frank. Compensating for their lack of

---

3   James A. Connolly, summary of statement. Connolly v. Prudential Arbitration.

experience, these conglomerates hired people like my father to steer their companies in the right direction.

With Gimbels, his objective was to regain market share in the game of catch-up they were playing with other retailers like Macy's. The company was stuck in a defensive position, and they were relying on their plan to expand into malls to make up for some lost ground. What they missed was how strongly a new phenomenon, "stagflation," can affect an already strained economy. As the nation's economy struggled to claw itself out of the pit carved by the Vietnam War, all while battling an oil crisis and social upheaval, interest rates and inflation were soaring to astronomical rates. High inflation and interest rates are usually associated with high economic growth, yet in this era growth had stagnated. The late 1970s marked an economic phenomenon never before seen in the history of the country.

Even with all of his qualifications, Jim Connolly represented a risk to Gimbels. Back then, companies were not hiring nonmerchants to fill such a pivotal position. He was a finance guy, called to lead the entire organization. The company understood they needed help getting their expenses under control. The position itself did not carry much longevity, but still, he walked in the door with a motive.

Deferring his salary was part of his plan to finance his own business. Even with a definitive end in sight, he still gave Gimbels 100 percent. While he was there, he managed to cut the company's shrinkage by record numbers. In 1978, he reduced shortages by a total of $3 million, implementing processes that would continue to serve the business in the years to come.

Unfortunately, he was only able to serve two out of the three contracted years when yet another restructuring led to the termination of his agreement. As a man of principle, Jim Connolly would never allow himself to waste time, especially not with so much on the line. He could sense things were not right, so he began to prepare for change, even before the need actually surfaced.

As I mentioned earlier, sometimes change can appear at the most inopportune time. When that happens, you just need to be ready to adapt and figure it out.

ABOVE ALL ELSE, REMAIN HUMBLE

> ... In a telephone interview, Elliot J. Stone, chairman and chief executive officer of Gimbels New York, called the resignation "a mutual parting of the ways that didn't happen suddenly" ... Mr. Connolly "now wants to do something different and we want at the same time to run this business with a little different structure." ...
>
> —*New York Times*
> **February 28, 1979**

Jim Connolly made a strong reputation for himself across the retail world and yet somehow still managed to remain a humble man. Back then, the decision to shift into entrepreneurship was not taken as lightly as it is today, especially at age fifty-eight, it was unheard of!

No longer president of a major company with all the perks that came with it, my father faced a dilemma. After weighing his options, he decided it did not make sense to try to work his way back into the retail industry, especially not after all he had done to prepare himself for the final leg of his journey. The time was finally here, but before he could get on with his mission, he had to conquer a few personal fears.

He sat on his plans for a few months. He needed time to calculate his next move. The discoveries that helped me piece together his story showed me that, during his hiatus in the fall of 1978 and winter of 1979, my father confided in a few of his former colleagues to get their opinions about whether or not it was right for him to move forward with his decision.

To be honest, his hesitation was justified. The retail climate was in turmoil at the time. There were mergers and acquisitions taking place left and right. Major brands were filing Chapter 11 just to try to salvage what was left of their business. The market was unstable, and at his age, my father was not exactly a first-round draft pick for some of these businesses that needed help.

He had already worked himself up to become president of a multimillion-dollar corporation. He knew what came along with the territory. The idea of going back was not appealing to him. At least not as appealing as building his own business.

Besides, any job he would have accepted would have slashed his salary. Working backward was not Jim Connolly's idea of success, so the more he weighed his options, the more it seemed like there was only one feasible direction. It was time to take a leap of faith and believe in himself once again.

Looking back, I have a newfound level of appreciation for my father's decision.

It took a certain level of humility for him to leave the glory of the corporate world behind. Suddenly, there was not a secretary around to handle mundane tasks like copying, filing, and sorting documents. He no longer had the safety of a steady salary to rely on. He went from commuting into NYC by train to driving himself on ninety-minute commutes that took him back and forth over the George Washington Bridge to his first client.

No more enviable office spaces with fine décor. Now he was operating out of my brother Larry's bedroom in our family house in Rye, New York. Once he made the decision to enter the paid bill audit business, soon to be known as the recovery audit business, he let his expertise pave the way. Thanks to his formidable reputation and the familiarity he'd developed over the years, he was able to launch Connolly Consulting Associates (CCA) with the help of a noteworthy list of former colleagues.

All the pieces were there. He just needed to figure out how to make everything come together.

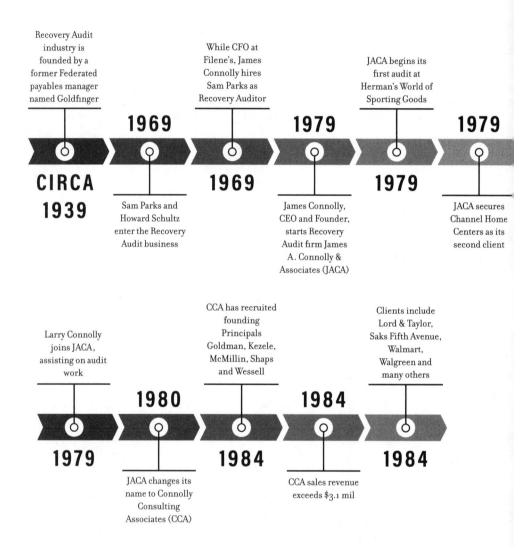

Recovery Audit industry is founded by a former Federated payables manager named Goldfinger

1969

While CFO at Filene's, James Connolly hires Sam Parks as Recovery Auditor

1979

JACA begins its first audit at Herman's World of Sporting Goods

1979

CIRCA 1939

1969

1979

Sam Parks and Howard Schultz enter the Recovery Audit business

James Connolly, CEO and Founder, starts Recovery Audit firm James A. Connolly & Associates (JACA)

JACA secures Channel Home Centers as its second client

CCA has recruited founding Principals Goldman, Kezele, McMillin, Shaps and Wessell

Clients include Lord & Taylor, Saks Fifth Avenue, Walmart, Walgreen and many others

Larry Connolly joins JACA, assisting on audit work

1980

1984

1979

1984

1984

JACA changes its name to Connolly Consulting Associates (CCA)

CCA sales revenue exceeds $3.1 mil

CHAPTER 2

Responding to the Call

Change Sets the Precedent for Greatness

This company was started from scratch on June 1, 1979, when James A. Connolly began alone to perform a postreview of paid media at Herman's World of Sporting Goods, Carteret, NJ. Three months later, with more than $100,000 in chargebacks processed (more than 85 percent of which was subsequently recovered) Connolly, ex-president of Gimbels New York and ex-CFO of Bloomingdale's and Filene's, had discovered

he enjoyed performing the work; the pay,
related professional contacts, activities,
and experiences could be very gratifying;
and he therefore decided to try to develop
a business in this area.

—James A. Connolly, *Connolly History 1979-84*

Change manifests itself in many different forms. There are planned, expected events as well as unforeseen opportunities we cannot afford to ignore. CCA began as a one-man operation. My father chose to cautiously approach the idea of forming his own business by doing what any good leader would do. He put himself in the trenches.

From 1979 to 1984, Jim Connolly built the foundation for a business that has stood the test of time. Five short years: that's all it took for him to become comfortable with the longevity of what he'd created. Five years fueled by a lifetime of determination.

THE RISE OF THE RECOVERY AUDIT INDUSTRY

When it comes to answering questions like why he got into the recovery audit business, I think it is best to let CCA's founder answer it himself:

Retail financial executives had long understood their accounts payable operations to
be massive paper-processing factories where
an army of clericals processed typically
ten thousand invoices in an average week,
from ten thousand possible vendors, cutting
across perhaps more than twenty-five
different industries, each with trade terms

slightly different from the others — and where each payment transaction, in order to be processed accurately, had to be matched and interpreted correctly in relation to at least three supporting documents: a purchase order, receiving receipt, and freight bill. An error or oversight in handling any one of many data-entry fields involved could trigger an overpayment. Even if the error rate in dollars was only .001, or .1 percent, for a retailer with $100 million in purchases annually, overpayments could add up to $100,000 — providing a nice recovery for the client and a nice payday for the auditor skillful enough to find and recover with a month or two of effort.[4]

CCA was created out of a blend of need and expertise. As CFO and president of some of the retail industry's top companies, Jim Connolly saw how lucrative this contingency fee industry could be. Using the industry norm error rate of one tenth of 1 percent (.1 percent), for a large retail company with annual purchases of, say, $1 billion, overpayments would be approximately $1 million. Today, sales of the retail sector are approximately $3.5 trillion, translating to roughly a $3.5 billion market for recovery auditing. It's not surprising my father eyed the opportunity before him with optimism.

Part of me wonders if he remembered how he was treated at Fowler, Dick & Walker. Despite how much he contributed or wanted to contribute, the family owners reaped the benefits, and there was

---

4   James A. Connolly, summary of statement. Connolly v. Prudential Arbitration.

nothing he could do about it. I don't necessarily believe he felt that reality was unjust, but I do think it helped him understand the value of ownership versus contribution, which ultimately influenced him to go at it on his own.

Though it's purely speculation, I would go as far as to say my father understood that, even with all the praise and accolades that come along with being an executive, his children would never inherit his New York City office, and he couldn't sign over his presidential perks in his will. In order to create a legacy, you sometimes must challenge yourself beyond your own expectations. Documents from my father's desk further explain why he took a risk on this industry:

Starting a business in this field was attractive to me for several reasons:

1. Low capital investment — mostly an ability to pay your bills until the cash began to flow in.

2. Retailing in the late '70s / early '80s had suffered subpar ROI for twenty years and thus was one of the first industries to feel the pressure for merger and acquisition, restructuring, downsizing, etc. As a result, there was readily available a supply of highly experienced financial executives at all levels of senior responsibility.

3. Because of the way the department store industry had been organized, my highly visible role therein for thirty years, plus

my personal reputation for competence and integrity, enabled me relatively quickly and easily to recruit an ample base of clients and associates.

4. Because of the nature of the work and the personal status of my associates, the endeavor was a natural to be organized on an independent contractor basis, which was very attractive to me personally.[5]

The attractiveness of the independent contractor model was coupled with the industry's standard contingency payment structure. Recovery auditing created minimal overhead costs, and without salaried employees, contingency payments meant everyone would only be paid for what was, essentially, "recovered."

There were no payroll expenses. No employment taxes or healthcare coverage. The benefit of this industry was in the auditor's ability to dig as deep as they could to recover as much money as possible, benefiting the client, the individual, and the company. For a man venturing out to follow an uncertain dream, the low risk, high reward of recovery auditing translated into an enticing opportunity.

In its inception, the recovery auditing industry was christened "the Goldfinger business," due to the pioneering efforts of a former payables manager of one of the Federated Department Stores in New York City, Mr. Goldfinger. He and his son-in-law were already setting a standard that challenged whether there was a place for small independent operations like CCA.

That Goldfinger had held a monopoly within the industry for

---

5   James A. Connolly, summary of statement. Connolly v. Prudential arbitration.

about thirty years was no secret. That is, until Sam Parks—yes, the same Sam Parks who was befriended by my father back in Cincinnati—and another gentleman by the name of Howard Schultz entered the field in 1969.

> *The mutual respect, both personal and professional, developed in these years endured and affected subsequent development of many careers, especially second careers in postpayment auditing. When Sam decided to enter the field in 1969 as CFO at Filene's, I was his first client, as Marty Goldman, then CFO of Lazarus, was the first client in that same year for Howard Schultz, our former colleague at Sanger-Harris.*[6]

Sam and my father only shared an apartment for a short amount of time, but they parted ways with a lifelong friendship. As S. H. Parks, Sam's recovery auditing business, began to expand, he approached my father in hopes of recruiting him as an auditor for the field. Sam offered[7] my father 10 percent of any account he helped the company retain, less his travel expenses, which was somewhere around the industry norm. However, my father had a plan, a vision all his own.

Rather than work for someone else, my father saw entrepreneurship as a much more lucrative option. He knew the industry. He had the connections. He'd built the reputation needed to gain people's trust. Sam's offer was not necessarily insulting, but my father was not prepared to settle. He'd worked his way to the threshold of what most people considered retirement age. If he planned to enjoy his golden years by his standards, then he could not spare any more time creating value for others. The time had arrived for him to build his own organization.

---

6   James A. Connolly, statement written for Jim Kezele's obituary.

7   JAC offer letter from Sam Parks and Associates, April 4, 1979.

Reading over the letter my father received from Sam, I noticed his willingness to negotiate terms to get his dear friend on board, which proved these men still had the utmost respect for one another. However, with all things considered, the recovery auditing industry is a competitive business.

There are only so many accounts to audit and only so much money to recover. The risk/reward model that comes along with performing third-party recovery audits could be advantageous if you had the right skills, but it also required a level of patience and financial stability to keep you committed until the rewards materialized.

I believe those final executive experiences were exactly what my father needed to develop the confidence to take on this challenge. He used his industry connections to gain Herman's World of Sporting Goods as his very first client, successfully recovering $100,000 in only three months.[8] He did all the work on his own. He gathered the purchase orders and arranged all the files. Herman's only had a single copier in their accounts payable department, and they needed it for business during the day. To be as minimally invasive as possible, my father would drive back to the client on the weekends just to gain ground on this audit. From beginning to end, he worked to make the Herman's account as successful as possible. By the time he completed the first of his prized audit reports, it was apparent that he was on to something outstanding.

Eventually, he recruited my brother Larry as his audit assistant. Larry would also help with the driving back and forth to Herman's New Jersey headquarters. Those long drives allowed time to think through more important tasks, like expansion.

Jim Connolly was always working on something. His intuition was always speaking to him. Building a business required him to

---

8   *Connolly Consulting Associates, Inc. History 1979–84.*

wear multiple hats. Whether it was securing the next client, recruiting new associates, or perfecting client deliverables before they were sent off, my father was thorough and realized the devil really was in the details. This trait is what separated us from the competition. No matter the size of the audit engagement, my father recognized that every single client interaction was an opportunity for CCA to differentiate and demonstrate value.

While the market was far from saturated, Sam Parks and Howard Schultz had a ten-year head start. My father realized that to compete, he had to differentiate. He decided from the very beginning CCA would be easy to work with and transparent. He prioritized the customer relationship, even if it meant walking away from fees. So beyond the dollars CCA recovered, he gave each client a management report at the end of each assignment detailing the errors that had occurred and what could be done to fix them. From the beginning, my father taught us that customers mattered more than anything.

My father realized that to compete, he had to differentiate. He decided from the very beginning CCA would be easy to work with and transparent. He prioritized the customer relationship, even if it meant walking away from fees.

CCA chose the "tell them everything you know" path, while the competition opted for an opaquer approach. Competitors were concerned that revealing too much, giving the client the power to go back and correct errors, could mean less money to recover on the next audit. But for CCA, it was more about building trust by letting clients know we were there to help them improve their operation. CCA was not interested in hiding what we found or even how we discovered the improper payments. My father understood that change was constant and thus new payment errors would occur.

With companies growing and implementing new processes, controls, and systems to keep up with demands, constant change meant the propensity for error was not going to change. From day one, my father felt that the client value of the insights in a Connolly Management Report were often greater than the dollar value of the actual recoveries of any given audit.

A WINDOW OF OPPORTUNITY

My archive of letters, documents, and files took a different turn when I came across a remembrance written by my father in 1995 for the passing of yet another lifelong friend and one of the founding principals of CCA, Jim Kezele. He was the same supportive soul who had told my father what he needed to hear to move forward with his plans to start the business. The mutual respect these men shared is a testament to the importance of being an honorable person, one who moves with integrity, intent, and purpose.

They had discussed my father's future plans in early 1979. To think of what must've transpired during that conversation is nothing short of heartwarming. It seems as if my father went to Jim to share his concerns and reservations around starting his own business. In doing so, he exposed his vulnerabilities, trusting his dear friend to help him make the right decision.

Judging by the way my father spoke so highly of Jim Kezele, I imagine Jim reassured my father during their talk and reminded him of all he had accomplished in his career. Jim was a qualified source to confide in. Not only had he witnessed my father triumph in the retail sector, he could also offer recovery audit industry insight, having worked for Sam Parks while Sam's new company was building a name for itself in the early '70s. That is, before my father used his lasting connections to help Jim land a more suitable career at Filene's.

He speaks of their conversations in his dedication to Jim Kezele, but I can only wonder what was on my father's mind at the time. He was not simply taking on the risk of breaching a developing industry; he was consciously deciding to put everything he earned as an executive on the line: his status, his reputation, and the life he'd created for himself and his family. He was planning to reinvent himself, even though he was quickly approaching the age of retirement.

I imagine he approached Jim with a solid question: "Do I do this, or don't I?"

Aside from seeking assurance, my father was also interested in soliciting support from his peers as he launched his business. I can only surmise that he propositioned Jim with a promise along the lines of, "If I do decide to start this business, will you come join me when the time is right?"

After I read through my father's files, it became obvious this discussion with Jim was one giving him the edge he needed to brave entering the recovery auditing industry on his own. Thankfully, not only did Jim encourage my father to take the leap, he accepted his offer to one day join the company as well.

As the storyline advanced in 1979, Jim buttoned things up at Filene's while my father was at his desk working out the details for CCA. The company was officially launched in the spring of that year, with the success of the Herman's engagement a sign that he was headed in the right direction. Although things went well with his first assignment, my father's calculating nature caused him to cautiously consider his options. He made it clear to us at home that things would be different for a while, at least until we knew the business could sustain itself.

CCA, first known as James A. Connolly and Associates (JACA), was started on a shoestring. My father launched the business from my brother Larry's old bedroom, turning my mother red with frustration at having her household turned upside down. In an instant, life at 751 Forest Avenue in Rye, New York, changed right before our eyes.

For me, the most glaring difference was my father's consistent presence. I was a junior in high school, and now he was home more often than I had ever experienced in my life. For as long as any member of our family could recall, my father's work routine was a constant. He would wake up in the morning, take the train to the city, and return after a long, full day. Often, it was my responsibility to pick him up at the station in the evening, never a minute late! Now, things were different. He was around, a transition that took some adjustments for the entire family.

Aside from his disturbing my mother's "home karma," Christmas 1979 demonstrated the brunt of the change underway. My father, in all his executive glory, made it clear to us all that this would be the year without a present exchange, placing extra emphasis on the uncertainty of his entrepreneurial decision. As the baby of the family, I decided to fill the void via expression, a letter to my family reinforcing my love and appreciation:

> For the five very special individuals who have each had their own different impacts and influences on my life. You have molded me, yet you have let me fill in the gaps for myself. As a result, I am a strong and confident person. I wish to use my strength and confidence to express myself to my family. I love you all very much, and I wish each of you a very Merry Christmas.
>
> —Libby, Christmas 1979

When the window of opportunity opened, my father made his way through. It required sacrifice from all of us, but we trusted his direction.

I would assume that, at this point, the question of the hour is, Why did he do it? What pushed him over the edge? I will never know for sure, but it seems as if he recognized potential that was too good to ignore. Armed with a Rolodex of colleagues who were also Harvard MBAs, ready to respond at his beck and call, and a laundry list of associates with industry connections, all the pieces were on the board. My father's career allowed him to build relationships with some of the most brilliant minds in the business. Competitors like Goldfinger, Sam Parks, and Howard Schultz may have had a head start, but CCA focused on attracting quality talent. Jim Kezele, Dan Shaps, Marty Goldman, Bob Wessel, and Jim McMillin were the founding principals, and all were on board by 1984.

Since the independent contractor model had become the industry norm, my father could capitalize on a lucrative payment structure that absolved him from the need to front expenses while his contractors were on assignment. His mind was made up.

THE FIRST CLIENTS OF CCA

When he was the president of Gimbels New York, my father seemed to have it all. A big job in the big city came with a big lifestyle. He worked out of a beautifully decorated office in Herald Square. He was frequently invited to fancy lunches in the most exclusive clubs, mingling with some of the most successful men in the world.

Then he gave all of it up. He turned down the lifestyle and the events to build his business all by himself. Now he was traveling, driving himself over the George Washington Bridge for an hour-and-a-half commute to his first client—not exactly the most luxurious way for a former executive to earn his living. Still, he persisted.

Having Herman's World of Sporting Goods in Carteret, New Jersey, as his first client was nothing short of a major break. Had it not been for his connections and the reputation he'd built for himself in the corporate sector, he may not have had the opportunity to secure this first client, and from there, success led to more success.

His reputation preceded him in the most fortunate ways. It gave him a competitive advantage that allowed him to scale the business without borrowing money. Business loans would only mean the business would be building itself with debt. That strategy was out of the question. Despite the uncertainty of the future of CCA, and our first ever presentless Christmas, which was not necessarily the end of the world, there were many positives to consider.

At the end of the day, that first audit was a success! He found $100,000 in overpayments at Herman's, with an 85 percent recovery rate and a 50 percent fee rate for CCA.[9] It took him six weeks over the summer of 1979 with little to no overhead. In less than two months, he was well on his way toward surpassing his annual executive salary. All by himself.

His reputation preceded him in the most fortunate ways. It gave him a competitive advantage that allowed him to scale the business without borrowing money.

That was the test run. Next, it was time to start scaling.

Always proactive and immensely hands-on, my father secured our next client, Channel Home Centers. Like Herman's, Channel was another division of W.R. Grace Consumer Services. By this

---

9   *Connolly Consulting Associates, Inc. History 1979–84.*

point, he had recruited the help of my brother Larry as his audit assistant. At the time, Larry had recently graduated from college and was painting houses with friends while considering his next move to gain stable employment. If the business were to grow, my father was going to need help. He was not quite ready to start recruiting his colleagues, but it was important to have some manpower to keep the momentum going. Family seemed like the best place to turn for help. Considering he had just financed Larry's college tuition, it was an easy ask.

My father secured the Channel Home Centers account using the same successful methods as before. Through his industry connections, he was able to make his way through the door and used this as an opportunity to make better use of Larry's talents. My brother followed our father's lead and began to perform audit procedures on his own. With Larry handling more and more audit work, our dad was free to commit more time to securing new clients and interviewing potential principals to expand the business.

During the Channel audit, Larry advanced from auditing cash discounts to freight charges and then got exposure to rebates, an opportunity not explored during that first audit at Herman's. Under my father's wing, he learned the business through a specific audit process designed by my father. They soon understood that each client experience is different. Channel proved this with how much more accommodating they were in delivering their records. That is, until CCA started to find *too many* overpayments.

We were at a half million dollars in recoveries, meaning we were on track to earn $250,000 in fees for a few weeks of work, when Channel suddenly intervened, claiming they weren't ready for an audit and explaining they had not performed their annual reconciliations. Despite the work that had been done, the exposure that had been uncovered, and the contractual terms to which Channel had agreed, my father made the decision to walk away and not dispute the situation.

The Channel audit taught us a valuable lesson. Not just in client relations, but in how my father's level of integrity would forever define our approach to working with our clients. He wasn't going to fight the client for breaching our agreement. He was trying to build a business, and you don't do that by challenging your clients. He had a personal relationship with the controller who had hired him for the job, and he was focused on building a long-term relationship. He believed in win-win solutions to problem-solving versus win-lose confrontations. Because of this, my father agreed to walk away from the large recovery, and in return, CCA was invited back to do another audit at Channel. Plus we were given a quid pro quo. The Channel controller got us a new opportunity to audit its sister division, Handy City, headquartered in Atlanta. Larry successfully handled that assignment solo, and that opportunity ultimately led to our expansion in the Southeast. The Handy Dan and Home Depot accounts soon followed, along with our first grocery account, Certified Grocers of Ocala, Florida.

The business was expanding quickly, additional contracts were being signed, and eventually my father needed some more help.

There was Gerry Leone, who headed our second audit at Herman's, which, eventually, my brother Larry rejoined. Larry worked with Gerry until he earned enough money to put himself through business school. He soon left CCA for the Freeman School of Business at Tulane University in January 1981. By this point, it was clear that CCA had the potential to become a reputable force in the recovery auditing industry—and my father was busy recruiting his very own "dream team."

This is when my father's dear friend Jim Kezele reentered the picture. In 1980, the year that the business was officially incorporated, Jim left his position at Filene's, and all the comfort and security a salaried job entails, to join CCA as a principal. He was eventually based out of Florida and managed the Southeast client portfolio, but his first assignment was on the Zayre account. Zayre was large, and CCA's first mass merchandising account, based just outside of Boston. Around that same time, a few other key executives followed Jim Kezele and joined CCA.

Robert Fortunato left his position as an assistant controller at Gimbels and Bloomingdale's. So did J. K. Roos, formerly of AMC. And Bob Wessel, an executive from W. Grace in New York City. Jim McMillin, an ex-CFO at Stix, Baer & Fuller, Rike-Kumler, and Shilito, who would develop the West Coast with Gordon Dick, Ken Stock, and Richard Bates. Dan Shaps, ex-VP of finance and operations at Sanger-Harris, who would develop the Midwest. And Marty Goldman, who would manage accounts in the Northeast.

With Kezele, Shaps, McMillin, Goldman, and Wessel in place as principals, Jim Connolly had a frontline army comprising highly skilled executives dispatched throughout the country. Joining forces with this group meant CCA could benefit from the connections these credentialed individuals had developed over the years.

My father summarized the four years that followed his lone Herman's audit by stating that CCA "comprised more than twenty-five executives, almost all of whom carried for twenty or more years of senior line management responsibilities in numerous major national retail companies. It had thus far completed more than 250 engagements in all parts of the United States for its 100 clients ... Virtually all CCA clients previously had an ongoing relationship with one of the two or three well-established practitioners in the field of paid media review."

The client roster included well-known companies at the time like, as my father wrote, "Abraham and Straus, Lord & Taylor, Saks Fifth Avenue, Marshall Field, Nordstrom, The Gap, Williams-Sonoma, Kohl's, J. C. Penney, Montgomery Ward, Ben Franklin, Walmart stores, Walgreens, Ames department stores, Caldor, Wanamaker's, Higbee, Jamesway, Zayre, Hit or Miss, Dayton's, Eckerd Drug, and Home Depot, among others."

By the close of the fiscal year in 1981, CCA had logged $684,000 in revenue. By 1983, the business had grown to $1.8 million. The next year, it nearly doubled revenue again to $3.1 million. In five short years, things were taking off, and it was all thanks to the way these men valued their position, worked hard to earn the respect of clients, followed the Connolly way, and embraced the potential of the business model.

THE CONNOLLY BUSINESS MODEL

The contingency fee model drove everything in the recovery audit business. The client, not knowing what expenditures were made in error, saw the model as a way to return "profits" with absolutely no investment other than what little time it took to hire the recovery auditor and give them the files to audit. The dollars recovered were seen as profit since they went right to the bottom line. The model also drove our auditor compensation, where the "reward" of producing recoveries for the client was wholly driven by the "risk" of the hard work it took to find them.

As the lone employee and auditor on that first assignment, Herman's, my father split the recovered overpayments with the client fifty-fifty. Over time, the client fee percentages changed dramatically from those 50 percent days due to competition, ultimately settling below 20 percent and, in some cases, the single digits. However, the basic principle from the beginning was the more dollars recovered, the more both the client and CCA benefited.

One might think the contingency model would lead an auditor to simply "throw it against the wall and see if it sticks." In reality, there was a built-in incentive to do quality work that realized irrefutable recoveries for the client. If auditing was performed but no recovery made, then the auditor realized no economic benefit for the time invested. Spurious overpayment claims would only make vendors and clients unhappy and would ultimately result in a contract not being renewed. Very often, CCA validated overpayments with vendors before bringing them to the client. Writing bad claims was simply not worth it! Our Connolly mantra, "there is no money in a bad claim," says it all.

There must be a level of trust to operate under a contingency fee model. This is where my father's reputation came to serve us. He was known for being a man who did the right thing, even when no one was looking. Over time, clients came to know CCA as a company they could trust.

Our clients trusted us with their proprietary information and to interact with their suppliers and providers as if CCA were an extension of them. We trusted our clients to honor our terms, and our auditors and principals trusted us to compensate them for their hard work. At the end of the day, no one got paid unless our client was able to successfully recover the money we identified. Even when they did, there was always a waiting period beginning from the time our clients recovered the funds from the vendor to the time they processed our payment. In the beginning, the clock did not start until *after* the entire audit was finished.

On the surface, the model appeared to be simple and relatively low risk, but it still created its own problems. On the front end, it kept our auditors incentivized to work harder to find as much money as possible, but it also placed us at risk too. As time went on, we had to navigate unexpected challenges like companies filing Chapter 11 before our fees were recovered, or clients like Channel, who needed us to walk away from work that we had done to avoid an embarrassing internal situation, or others where we had to avoid creating a relationship problem with an important supplier.

My father's team of skilled principals and audit associates was spread throughout the country. The rapid growth of CCA was proof that his business model was working. Working on contingency fee can be risky: no findings, no fees. But we had a couple of things going for us. One of our greatest assets was our "low-noise" approach to our client work, the other was our fee-sharing structure.

THE LOW-NOISE APPROACH

CCA did its best to be as minimally invasive toward the client as possible. We called this a low-noise approach. My father set the standard when he was willing to sacrifice his weekends to get his work done at Herman's, thereby not interfering with the client's weekday activity. Then he raised the bar when he walked away from Channel without a fight. From the very beginning, there was never any confusion: put your clients' interests first. Jim Connolly showed us how to look at the bigger picture.

You do not rock the boat with clients, no matter how the situation unfolds. You listen to what they need and strategize accordingly. Above all else, you remind yourself that your relationship with the customer comes before anything else. If things don't go as planned, use that situation to open some other door. CCA never wanted to disrupt our clients' operations or their relationships with their suppliers and providers. To secure long-term relationships, we made it our goal to help clients recover improper payments—money they hadn't realized they'd lost—and act as an extension of their team.

One of the reasons why the low-noise approach was so successful was because of how transparent we were throughout the process. Our openness was the strategy that set us apart from our competitors. We didn't hide information from our clients, and my father saw to it that every single client management report was flawless.

We were sure to include detailed descriptions of what we did, how we did it, what we discovered in the process, and how it might be fixed in the future. This let our clients know that CCA was a company they could trust, earning repeat business, wonderful client relationships, and glowing recommendations for many years. Job security!

Those recommendations were as good as gold, considering how we also understood that getting a new client was much more difficult than nurturing an existing relationship. By focusing on long-term objectives, we were rewarded with significant achievements. From the late '90s onward, which is when we started tracking, our client retention rate was near spotless, and we were operating at about 97 percent client satisfaction as measured by an independent survey. By the time we moved into healthcare, client retention was 100 percent (from 1998 to 2014). But we will get to that maverick of a story in a minute.

Despite the challenges the model presented, we remained true to our values and continued with our low noise and transparency strategy. My father didn't see the benefit in omitting information and selectively disclosing what we found. To him, there was no reason to fear a client correcting issues we had identified, which would eliminate the need for future work. He understood change was constant and change would create new opportunities for recovery. Besides, even if that happened, it would not be the first time he worked himself out of a job. He'd taken on a volunteer kamikaze mission before!

The foundation of our payment structure was rooted in integrity. And, as my father has always iterated, through hard work and unbendable moral fiber, we would *always* secure another client based upon our reputation and track record.

PAYING OUR PEOPLE: CONNOLLY'S FEE-SHARING MODEL

Another component of our business model was the extension of the contingency-fee structure, and it impacted the way we paid our people. My father believed that the most productivity would come from people with skin in the game. When he was working alone, there were no fees to share, and things were simple, but as the company began to expand, a payment structure had to be established to accommodate the principals and auditors that were working in the field.

At the outset, here is how it worked. For every fee dollar received from the client, the structure went as follows:

- 50 percent went to the auditor(s) performing the work

- 25 percent went to the principal

- 10 percent went to whomever initially sold the account (either CCA or the principal)

- 15 percent went to CCA

Of course, all of this was after direct expenses such as copying, supplies, and office expenses. As time went on and the business evolved, and as more principals, senior auditors, auditors, and support staff were brought on, the structure saw several adjustments. But what never changed was the spirit of the structure, which was to reward those producing recoveries for the client. Aligning risk with reward was critical to attracting the talent needed to produce results for our clients. And for many of our principals and auditors, the reward could be very lucrative, more than offsetting the risk.

By the end of 1984, the business model had paid off. CCA had completed over 250 assignments for one hundred clients, earning $3.1 million in revenue. Our payment and fee structure may have evolved, but we stuck to our guns as we expanded, continuing to align risk with reward. Our business growth was methodical: one client at a time. No outside investment. No acquisitions. Just hard work and a determination to be the best by delivering quality results with low noise.

One client at a time. No outside investment. No acquisitions. Just hard work and a determination to be the best by delivering quality results with low noise.

In the coming years, we continued to honor the compensation model that rewarded CCA so handsomely. As the business grew, roles and responsibilities were eventually changed, but we were smart enough to figure out how to modify our compensation structure within the model that'd been tried and tested. My father handed us a great business model, and there was no denying its advantages. Sticking to it is one of the reasons why we managed to remain so successful.

Most importantly, we continued to rely on the "figure it out" mentality my father used to get the business off the ground. After proving to be so consistent, transparent, trustworthy, and efficient, Jim Connolly left behind some pretty big shoes to fill. Soon the time would come for my brother and me to carry the business on our own.

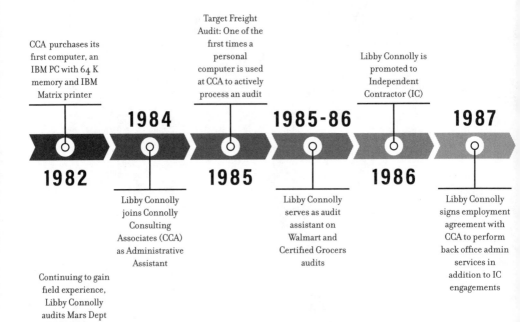

CCA purchases its first computer, an IBM PC with 64 K memory and IBM Matrix printer

Target Freight Audit: One of the first times a personal computer is used at CCA to actively process an audit

Libby Connolly is promoted to Independent Contractor (IC)

1984

1985-86

1987

1982

1985

1986

Libby Connolly joins Connolly Consulting Associates (CCA) as Administrative Assistant

Libby Connolly serves as audit assistant on Walmart and Certified Grocers audits

Libby Connolly signs employment agreement with CCA to perform back office admin services in addition to IC engagements

Continuing to gain field experience, Libby Connolly audits Mars Dept Stores, Ames , NYNEX, Abraham & Straus and Montgomery Ward

1986-90

CHAPTER 3

Take the Risk

Calculating Your Next Steps

*Taking calculated risks means being thoughtful about
why you are taking the risk, what you hope to achieve,
and why you think your goal is possible.*

—Libby Connolly Alexander

M y brother Larry and I are six years apart in age, with
me being the youngest of the family. Larry graduated
college in 1979, and I graduated from high school the
very next year. By the summer of 1980, I was packed
and on a plane to New Orleans to pursue a liberal arts education at

Tulane University.

Seeing me go was not easy for my mother. We moved around a lot over the years, from Wilkes-Barre, Pennsylvania, to Cincinnati, Ohio, Wellesley, Massachusetts, and Rye, New York. Me being the last child to leave the nest left her to accept the fact that even more changes were happening at home.

By the time I went to Tulane, CCA had been up and running for a year. I saw a lot of the hustle and bustle during those first few months, but after I left, that's when things really started taking off. After Larry graduated from Washington and Lee University, he was home for a while, but overall, my mother's four children were off living their own lives.

That isn't to say this was an easy time for any of us.

Ronald Reagan was just elected president of the United States, and the nation was facing the impact of soaring interest rates and unimaginable rates of inflation. Unlike today, it wasn't the most opportune era for liberal arts majors to be entering the job market. Larry found that out quickly, and after gaining some professional experience while working with our dad, and a nice salary in the process, it made sense for him to round out that experience with an advanced degree.

The economy quickly taught most liberal arts majors that continuing their education in either law school or by pursuing their MBA was the only way they'd manage to secure a well-paying job. So that's exactly what my brother did.

I was in the middle of my freshman year when Larry landed in New Orleans to enroll at Tulane's Freeman School of Business for his graduate studies. You can imagine how popular I became as the sister of a "cool" B-School student. It didn't take long for my friends to make friends with his buddies. From January 1981 to May

1982, we were in New Orleans together. Neither of us were award-winning academics—not terrible, but not magna cum laude types either. Nonetheless, having him there with me in New Orleans was a great experience.

With CCA still getting off the ground, money continued to be tight back home. My father was generous enough to cover my tuition and room and board, but I was on the hook for everything else. So I found a few ways to take care of myself.

I had various part-time jobs while at school, from working retail in the French Quarter at Dansk and Laura Ashley to working the door at Tyler's, a well-known jazz club where oysters were sold for ten cents and served by the dozens on brown plastic lunch trays with the best jazz New Orleans had to offer. I was also on the Tulane sailing team, so I was pretty busy most of my days. I performed well enough to get by and learned all I could while I tried.

At the end of my sophomore year, I went back home, and Larry stayed in New Orleans. He was working at a business called ComputerLand, following along with the rest of the country's newfound fascination with personal computing.

Interestingly enough, I did not go back to Tulane for my junior year. Instead of traveling abroad, I spent a year in Washington, DC, thanks to my mother's prodding. I enrolled at Trinity College, a quaint all-girls' Catholic school in the northwest part of the capital and continued my studies. Simultaneously, I held an internship for Senator Daniel Patrick Moynihan, one of the longest-serving senators for the state of New York, who also held cabinet or subcabinet positions for Presidents Kennedy, Johnson, Ford, and Nixon. He was an ambassador to India as well as to the United Nations.

Amid so many changes taking place in my academic and professional spheres, tragedy struck in January of my junior year while I was home on holiday break. I received the devastating news that my high school best friend, Feffi Stiassni, had passed away. Her passing hit me hard. It reminded me that life is short. As a last-minute decision, I opted for adventure and headed back to Washington, which led to an internship at the US Supreme Court, doing genealogical research on its founding members.

My experiences in Washington were valuable for many reasons. Perhaps most importantly, I learned to be independent and willing to take on new opportunities as they came my way. This was exactly what my mother would have wanted. She was a strong advocate for her daughters and wanted my sister and me to be afforded the same opportunities as my father, opportunities she never knew. Though I had not quite found my place, I made sure to put forth my best in whatever project I was working on. Little did I know at the time how this experience would help me down the road as I took on more and more responsibility at CCA.

For my senior year, I made my way back to Tulane, majoring in history. I had decided to drop French as a double major, which freed up a few credit spaces for me. So I enrolled in a basic computer coding class, an elective that would serve me and CCA for many years.

I can remember my first experience with a personal computer. Without disclosing my age, I can make it known that things were considerably different back then. As a history major, I had a ton of papers to write to fulfill my graduation requirements. Between the exposure offered through computer coding and my desire to get my reports written as efficiently as possible, I got comfortable with the computer lab on campus.

I challenged myself. Instead of typing my finals out on the type-writer, battling rogue ribbons, misalignments, and tubs of Wite-Out,

I wanted to use a word processor to sort them out. Word processors were precursors to the personal computer, dedicated strictly to handling documents. The task presented a learning curve for me, but it was not supremely difficult to overcome. When I considered the alternative, I was motivated to start piecing the puzzle together.

To my surprise, word processors were incredibly efficient! I was exposed to the unexpected while on the brink of the classic liberal arts experience. My eyes were opened to the possibility of what technology could bring to the table. Now that I saw the possibility, it was time to put my elective knowledge into action.

JOINING THE FAMILY BUSINESS

"Look, I've got this thing going, and I could use your help."

This about sums up how I was inducted into the business. It was July 1984, I was still in New Orleans, a recent graduate of Tulane. Even in New Orleans, which for us Northerners felt like a different country, I was not exempt from the impact of the nation's stressed unemployment rate, which while I was in college had broken into double-digit range for the first time since the Great Depression. I received a call from my father while working at the World's Fair, one of the last of these famous events to be hosted in the country. I was working at the electric energy exhibit back then, but after I got that call, my next steps were clear. My father had spoken.

"Look, I've got this thing going, and I could use your help."

Les bon temps were over. It was time to get home and get serious.

He didn't give me much of a choice, either. While evaluating all he had invested into his children over the years and what he was developing within his business, my father figured it was time to collect on a few debts. He had already financed my and Larry's college tuitions; now it was time for us to give *him* some support.

I was initially hired on to assist with administrative tasks at the "corporate headquarters," our family house in Rye, New York. I helped in the office (Larry's former bedroom) while learning my way around the business. Above all else, I learned my father was a great teacher. But first, I had to humble myself.

I was an employee, just like anyone else. Despite what some of our independent contractors may have believed, my father was never lax with Larry and me because we were his children. When I think about it, I went from having my fancy New York debutante cotillion, being featured in this grand party, to having my desk put in a closet in a bedroom in our house a couple of feet from the man I was now working for, my father. There were not any silver spoons being passed around. He had a full plate, and a lot of people were depending on him.

My first few tasks were easy enough: basic bookkeeping and banking.

Thanks to an accounting course I'd taken in college with legendary Tulane Business School and accounting professor Beau Parent, I was not completely unfamiliar with the process. Still, I had to learn to do these things according to the standard set by Jim Connolly. That meant it was time to roll up my sleeves.

On the banking side, my job was to deposit checks the minute they arrived. That was the top priority. My father had the delivery services timed and knew exactly when the mail was supposed to arrive. Whenever we received a check, the starting gun sounded. You'd snatch envelopes out of the mailbox and rush to the bank. When it came to distributions, paying commissions to our auditors and principals, there was no time to waste.

The money coming through the door needed to be turned around quickly and distributed to those doing the work. Those deposits are what enabled us to pay our independent contractors in a timely manner. My father made sure I understood I held more than a piece of paper in my hands. Those checks represented people's livelihoods, their ability to keep a roof over their heads and dinner on the table. Turning the money around quickly reflected on my father's business efficiency and helped him develop trust with his associates. And after absorbing months of expenses on their own, let's just say people were happy to see a tan envelope arriving from Connolly Consulting.

My father made sure I understood I held more than a piece of paper in my hands. Those checks represented people's livelihoods.

I took on the task of deposits and distributions like someone's life was on the line. Because it was. My next assignment, though, carried even more significance.

Before long, my father "promoted" me to help handle our client management reports. If you recall, these reports, given to our clients at the conclusion of an audit, were *the* differentiator between us and the bigger guys. The fact that my father trusted me to read through, proofread, and check for errors in these lengthy, sometimes twenty-plus-page reports trained me painfully to pay attention to details.

These reports were a major component of CCA's value proposition. Not only did they tell our clients about the dollars we recovered, they informed them about weaknesses in their processes and systems. We followed up with applicable recommendations for them to improve processes moving forward. If they implemented those recommendations, we essentially solved their overpayment problems for them.

My dad gambled that this advice, despite its tremendous value, would not be fully implemented by the client. He deductively reasoned that other factors, like cost constraints and competing priorities, would prevail. Therefore, the threat of cannibalizing the recovery opportunity for subsequent assignments would be minimal. The flip side of this thinking was the trust and goodwill he established with clients by going beyond the numbers and sharing what he knew.

Everything in these reports needed to be accurate. The figures had to be correct, and everything had to be spelled correctly. These reports were like book-sized business cards for Connolly, so I had to deliver.

Though it may have been a bit overwhelming at first, this responsibility actually started to serve me while I worked. This was grunt work to be sure, but reading over these reports began to teach me the business. I learned the language. I familiarized myself with the types of errors our auditors would find. Essentially, these reports became the training manual that helped me prepare for my next assignment.

With each challenge thrown my way, I was taught one of the greatest skills anyone can have in the world of business: reliability. I realized how many people were counting on me to do this and do it right. A mistake on my end could mean that someone did not get paid on time or, even worse, that our reputation could be damaged. I was not going to let that happen. So I developed the behaviors needed to become as reliable, and accurate, as possible.

THE IBM PC

Every time we received a check, our integrity was placed on the line. That meant dropping everything to get the job done. I had to be responsive. Timeliness was one of my main job requirements.

Saturday afternoons ... so what? If we got a check, I dropped every-thing and made my way to the bank, and I still was not done.

That job took on a second part: bank reconciliations. We were still working at the time with paper ledgers, just as my father had when he first started his career. I still have one dating back to 1980. Back then, CCA operated on somewhat of a dual accounting system, logging cash receipts, disbursements, and expenses manually in Boorum & Pease hardcover columnar ledgers, then reentering them into our computer accounting package at the end of each month to create the financials.

I mean, it was as old school as you can get—a black hardcover accounting ledger with a maroon binding. Inside had grid paper with columns. First, I had to complete all our entries. Then, when Larry sold CCA our first IBM PC, my father added Peachtree's accounting package to the list. Performing all those back entries on a testy accounting system was not an easy task. My father did not sympathize; instead, he insisted it was necessary.

"You always run things in parallel because, if you can't reconcile, you can go back and find the error."

Always have a redundant system. I believe the strategy was probably gifted to him through business school and all the computer implementations he oversaw at Federated. For him, the greatest incentive for teaching me how to run these operations was the fact that he did not have to do them anymore!

"You always run things in parallel because, if you can't reconcile, you can go back and find the error."

Some may believe that you can only measure someone's professional competency through their ability to perform complex tasks.

But greater challenges are not the true measuring stick of success; it is how well you can handle the simple and mundane with accuracy.

Even with systems in place, accounting and banking require refined attention to detail. Things like management reports and data entry can be thrown off just by one overlooked digit.

Keep in mind, long before the average man, woman, and child walked around with a handheld supercomputer in their purse or back pocket, PCs were strictly designed for businesses. It was not until people realized the benefits PCs could present outside of the workplace did interest reach its peak. This was known as the "micro-computing revolution" in the '80s.

The growing demand paved the way for the formulation of companies like ComputerLand, which was chosen as one of the outlets to first introduce the IBM PC, creating a retail environment for consumer purchases. To compare this turn of events to more recent phenomena, consider the attention drawn around the release of the World Wide Web or touchscreen mobile devices, for my postinternet readers.

PC games were enough to raise a few eyebrows at first. Then came the inclusion of various floppy disc drives and software programs that helped the average user—or, in our case, budding family business—do things more efficiently.

Working at ComputerLand, Larry managed to secure a 38 percent discount for the purchase of CCA's first computer. Using his expert negotiating skills, he explained the value an IBM PC could bring to the business, as well as how it would help him complete his business school courses. All in all, he required a $2,978 investment from my father, which isn't a small sum in any era, particularly not in the early '80s. Computers hadn't fully proven their worth, but my father trusted my brother's advice, and he was willing to accept the fact that change was on the horizon.

When the PC arrived, I had to use all the raw computer-programming skills I had gained from that elective at Tulane University to work with the database program dBASE to get the machine to operate as we needed it to. Taking an off-the-shelf program and making it work for CCA put all my "figure it out" abilities to the test. It took a few attempts, but I figured it out.

THE TARGET MANIFEST AUDIT

In the spring of 1985, while I was doing banking and administrative work for CCA, I offered to help Marty Goldman, principal, perform a freight audit for Target, our latest client, from Minneapolis, Minnesota. He needed help identifying shipments made within the New York commercial-free zone where Target was charged for shipping. If I could find any improper freight charges, I was to issue a chargeback so Target could collect the erroneous payments. After studying the work to be done, I decided to enlist the latest version of dBASE, called dBASE III.

Lou Levine, who was an audit associate on the account, sent all the shipping manifests to me in Rye, and this became the first time our PC was used to actively process an audit. I used the computer to log data from the manifests, then sort and print vendor schedules that listed all the incorrect freight charges. From there, we were able to process vendor chargebacks and collect the overbilled freight charges.

Marty Goldman helped with the photocopying of my printed computer schedules. Lou Levine drafted the chargebacks and submitted them to the client for deduction. I went over everything with an eagle eye. By the completion of the audit, we identified $234,766 in improper freight charges, netting $177,622. Of this, CCA earned $78,811 in fees. Not bad for my first assignment!

For my efforts, I received two bonuses—$1,500 each from both Mr. Levine and Mr. Goldman, and then $2,000 from CCA. Later, I received an additional $1,000 from Mr. Goldman and an additional $1,000 from CCA.

Mind you, my earnings were also meant to cover the $1,300 I spent to purchase the dBASE III software and other expenses that CCA did not compensate me for. While working on the project, the software continuously crashed, most times just as I was completing my data-entry tasks. Frustrated, I ended up traveling to the ComputerLand store in Stamford, Connecticut, to complete my assignment using a floor model machine. I needed to figure it out and get the job done, correctly, by any means.

Managing to sort out the bugs on the computer in the store, I realized CCA's computer was in desperate need of an upgrade. We were struggling to process bigger volumes of data, and stagnated performance was not efficient. I took it upon myself to get what was needed to fix the problem going forward.

In many ways, taking on the Target assignment was a calculated risk on my part. From my experience, I trusted that a computer could be used to get the job done more efficiently. I knew it could help us automate the tasks involved, making the out-of-pocket investment worth it. Although I didn't have the title, I was in effect acting as an auditor, including taking on the expense to perform the work myself.

CCA made calculated steps toward advancement by scaling up slowly. Whenever we tried something new, we had to figure it out first.

This is a prime example of yet another recurring theme found within our business. CCA made calculated steps toward advancement by scaling up slowly. Whenever we tried something new, we worked to figure it out first. We didn't need to be 100 percent certain about the success that would come, but we needed enough evidence to calculate the risk at hand to see if it was worth the reward.

I may have footed the bill on my own, but my resourcefulness did not go unnoticed. Receiving my first review as a Connolly associate really set things into stone:

> Our goal for your first year was for you to become familiar with and competent in all of the systems and procedures we use in operating and controlling CCA, Inc. I couldn't be more pleased with your actual performance against these goals. You have mastered all of the basic bookkeeping and other record keeping, correspondence, filing, report editing and production, bank reconciliation, etc. procedures in the business to the point where for a long time now, I have felt confident in your ability to handle routine transactions with virtually no supervision. In addition, I have especially noticed the high level of enthusiasm with which you usually perform your tasks, and the spirit of dedication and responsibility with which you have frequently worked evenings, weekends, and holidays, when necessary, to get work done on a prompt and timely basis.[10]

By the time my father wrote my review, I'd been working for CCA

10   Libby Connolly Alexander's annual performance review, July 1985.

for nearly a year, and I was ready for the next challenge. I still had to prove myself; that was understood. In the eyes of the principals, I was Jim Connolly's daughter, so they expected me to move with a sense of entitlement. Larry would always remind me that because of who I was, I had to work harder than everyone else. So I did.

I didn't have to take on the Target audit, but I recognized the need. One of my primary focuses has always been on helping the business run more efficiently. I took the initiative, and things paid off. It gave my father the confidence to continue to allow me to test the waters.

The prospect of getting in my car and driving myself out to a place called Bentonville, Arkansas, was not the most exciting idea in the world.

It gave me a boost in confidence too. While I was still receiving an administrative salary, my father next sent me on the road. I was not quite sure where I would fit in the business, but he was concentrating on the bigger picture. The prospect of getting in my car and driving myself out to a place called Bentonville, Arkansas, was not the most exciting idea in the world. However, my father felt like putting me on the large Walmart account, as Larry's audit assistant, was the best place for me to get my feet wet in the field.

THE WALMART AUDIT: ASSUMING THE ROLE OF LARRY'S AUDIT ASSISTANT

With Dan Shaps's Walmart account contributing $1 million in revenue by this point in our company's history, the first time we'd breached the million-dollar mark in a single audit, and with plenty of other noteworthy clients entering the conversation, this was an exciting time for the company.

Just to paint the picture for you, Bentonville circa 1985 was nothing like the Bentonville there is today. Walmart was still relatively small and not the mega-successful company it now is. Back then I was driving to the Middle of Nowhere USA, and it didn't exactly feel worth it in the beginning.

I'll never forget how at one point of the audit, I needed to fly home, and to get to an airport, I either had to drive to Missouri or Oklahoma. There was no commercial airport in Bentonville.

This time, I chose to fly out of Missouri, and while I was trying to find what I thought would be a reasonably large airport, I drove right past it! Tucked between towering cornfields and walls of wild foliage, the tiny rural airport was almost invisible.

Remember, I was in my twenties at the time. Living in a condo with Larry in Bella Vista, northwestern Arkansas, left much to be desired in the realm of social stimulation. There was one bowling alley and one bar, and the town was so tight knit, everybody knew everyone. This meant, as outsiders, we stuck out like a sore thumb.

For a girl who had just graduated and moved out of New Orleans and Washington, DC, Bentonville was serving up heaping helpings of culture shock. It was different. Not to mention, all my friends were exploring their youth, living urban '80s lifestyles in places like New York City, Boston, or some other "happening" area. Wherever they were, they certainly weren't anywhere near Bentonville.

Alas, that was the path I chose for myself. Sitting in a warehouse in rural Arkansas. No formal office space. No official setup. We did our work on folding brown tables, with a warehouse of boxes and a heart full of ambition. That's it.

We humbly approached our work in the simplest way with these hallmark brown tables. I was Larry's audit assistant. My job was to organize all the documents he needed to perform a vendor review and then create schedules of his findings. We had boxes of old files being passed down a makeshift assembly line, working through Walmart's records as a team. Anyone who did not have a level of humility by the time they got to Bentonville got it very quickly.

My father impressed upon us the importance of understanding the business from the ground up, another one of his philosophies that we took to heart as we scaled the business. By the time Larry and I took over the leadership of CCA, we had each spent seven years in the field working various client assignments. From this experience, we understood that the company's main job was to support auditor innovation and the success of our audit engagements. It was simple: if the audits were successful and made money, the company would be successful and make money. We took this to heart. Later on, when we hired our first corporate employees, we sent everyone out into the field, regardless of their position. Even our first VP of human resources went to the field. We called it boot camp. We understood there is no way you can properly lead or manage a company if you do not understand first what your people are doing in the field.

Recovery auditing is something you must experience to fully appreciate. There's really no way to articulate what it is like to travel to these remote towns and isolate yourself for months on end, to foot your own expenses and work on contingency with no assurances of return on time invested. Conversely, there were the thrill and adrenaline rush that come with a finding a recovery and calculating commissions. It is unlike any other business I know.

MAKING GOOD ON HIS PROMISE

As I've contended throughout the progression of this memoir, I strongly believe my father was a man before his time. He saw value in me that superseded my gender, and he invested himself into helping me rise to my fullest potential.

"If you decide to stay and work for Connolly, I'll teach you everything they'd teach you at Harvard Business School."

It was ironic to hear a man with an MBA from Harvard convince me not to attend a business school myself. Nonetheless, my father presented me with an interesting proposition: go to graduate school, or stay on the job and immerse yourself in an experiential learning environment that just so happened to be earning me a lot of money.

The decision was not that difficult. I wasn't a great student to begin with and decided to forego the idea of taking entrance exams and going back to school. Instead, I spent my first two years with Connolly closely following my father's lead. He promised to teach me everything I needed to know, and as always, he delivered.

> *"If you decide to stay and work for Connolly, I'll teach you everything they'd teach you at Harvard Business School."*

By paying his wisdom forward, he saved me thousands of dollars in tuition. As I mentioned, I was a B student on my best day, so slugging away inside the classroom was not on the top of my priority list anyway. Working with CCA, I had the opportunity to learn while I earned, and that made much more sense to me.

Things kicked up a gear between 1985 and 1986. I started with a six-month investment on the Walmart account. When that assignment ended, I traveled back across the country straight to Ocala, Florida. Summertime in Florida was an experience in itself, but it did not outshine what it was like earning my keep under Jim Kezele.

Horse country in the Sunshine State was quite beautiful, but despite its picture-perfect landscapes, it was *still* in the middle of nowhere. Nevertheless, it was home to Certified Grocers, my next assignment.

While there, I lived with Jim's daughter in a mobile home in Gainesville, Florida, which sent this city girl for a loop. It was a trailer park. There is no way to jazz up this part of the story, but I needed a cheap room. I was on assignment for the next four months, and my dad presented a timely opportunity to rent her spare room. Noting my silent hesitance, he broke down the situation to me as plainly as it could get.

"You got any better ideas?"

Without much rebuttal, I signed up and was prepared to do what was necessary to get the job done.

My heart sank every time I backed up my car to the parking pad of grass beside that trailer. I knew it was 120 degrees inside, and our metal mobile home was just sizzling, baking under the unforgiving Floridian sun.

Several weeks in, I was on the verge of a meltdown, literally!

Bentonville was pretty bad, but this situation was almost unbearable.

I cannot tell you this was something I necessarily wanted to do, but I was learning and proving to myself I could handle this type of work. The trade-off was something I constantly questioned, between living conditions and being away from my then boyfriend, Robert, and my friends. Socially, I was miserable. My friends thought I had lost my mind. The grass always looks greener when you're standing on the other side. The decision didn't feel good, but I knew it was what I needed in my life at the time.

Complaining to Robert was out of the question. Every time I tried, he offered the same response: "Then why are you doing this? Just come home."

To him, quitting would instantly resolve my unhappiness, but I just could not do it. Connollys don't quit. We see things through to the end.

By the end of the summer, I officially earned my father's seal of approval, and he reevaluated the contribution I was making to the business. The certified audit was a success, and I guess he deduced that he had not sent me to college just to spend my days as an administrative assistant. My mother was not short on objections either.

Since I followed through on my word, I learned the desire for experience can drive one's willingness to get in the trenches and figure it out. I saw what could come from the decision to face your fears and make yourself uncomfortable, if only for a few months. I put my skills up against men who had years and years of exposure stamped on their resumes, and I learned from them. Regardless of my professional history or my age, over time I managed to use everything my father instilled in me to develop a level of mastery in the recovery auditing industry.

There was no doubting what I could do, and before long, my next assignment was evident. It was time for me leave the nest again. This time as an official independent contractor.

CONNOLLY CONSULTING ASSOCIATES, INC.
RETAIL OPERATIONS • SYSTEMS • FINANCIAL CONTROLS
CENTRAL OFFICE · BOX 14404
ST. PETERSBURG, FL 33733

813-867-3117

Aug 29, 1986

Mrs. Elizabeth Ann Connolly

Dear Libby:

Enclosed is CCA check # 1783 for $3,214.00 - your net (after $500 Federal Income Tax and $286 ZICA tax with holding) of your $4,000 gross pay-check for July and August 1986.

Confirming our telephone conversation early this week, this will terminate your services as an Administrative employee of CCA Inc. Henceforth your relationship with CCA Inc will be that of an Independent Contractor with exactly the same rights and obligations as all other CCA Independent Contractors — no more, no less — with which from your part experience you already are fully familiar. Enclosed is your written contract covering your new status. If agreeable with you, please sign original and return to me. The copy is for your records.

James A Connolly
President

AN INDEPENDENT CONTRACTOR

Unlike the majority of audit associates who worked for CCA, Larry and I were the only ones who did not have a tenured career in the retail finance function. Without that background, we were less credentialed than our counterparts, so my father made a way for us to fill that gap via work effort and results.

My contracted agreement clearly iterated statements from my father that were already expressly understood. I knew I was expected to perform the same duties as any other Connolly independent contractor, no more and no less. Others may have assumed we'd be able to flex some influence as the "boss's brats," but Larry and I knew better. That was never going to happen. No matter what role you held at CCA, my father viewed us all as equal extensions of his reputation.

Knowing this, I must say, receiving my promotion was a moment of mixed emotion. To be completely honest, after those two test runs on the road, the life of a traveling auditor did not seem as attractive as it had while I was doing the banking for the business and cutting lucrative commission checks. At first, I was drawn in by the compensation potential, but man, earning that money came with big personal sacrifices.

I had a lot to consider before I could commit. Thoughts of my friends and their seemingly more fun lives were still dancing around in my head. Then there was something else. A soft spot I haven't even addressed yet ...

SACRIFICES OF THE HEART

My relationship with Robert was another big wrinkle in this opportunity. Now married, back then we were twentysomethings who were head over heels in love. We met during my senior year in college, at a sailing regatta in Chicago. Rob was sailing for Boston University, and I was sailing for Tulane. New Year's Eve 1984 was our first date.

After graduation, Robert moved to New Orleans. He lived with me, my college roommate Frances Daniels, and her best friend from high school, Susan Geary. The three girls were working, while Robert tinkered all day with an old racing green Triumph Spitfire that he used to drive me back and forth to my job at the World's Fair. Post-graduation for all four of us, we worked all day and enjoyed the nightlife of the city. Summer shenanigans. Laissez les bon temps rouler.

Then my dad interrupted it all at the end of July with his call for help. I headed home, while Robert, never short on adventure, went to Hawaii to go windsurfing for a few months with one of his best mates, Andy Morrell. One of the smartest people I've ever met, Robert had figured out how to take advantage of interest-free loans the government was offering to students to pay for the trip.

When he returned, he found out what I'd agreed to do, and he thought I had lost my mind. He thought my father had orchestrated the deal on purpose, sending me to Bentonville just to keep us apart.

We were in love, and when you're young like that, you don't see any reason why you should not or could not be together.

Robert did not understand why I would make such a decision back then, especially when he was certain I could just find a job somewhere in New York or Connecticut near him. But I weighed my options, listened to my gut, and off I went.

Because of the lessons we learned from that experience, even to this day, we are always reminding our children of the importance of worrying about *yourself* first. Before love. Before your friends. Before other people's opinions.

Take care of yourself before all else. It is the only way you will ever guarantee your own happiness.

Before what you've deemed as your responsibility to the next person. Take care of yourself before all else. It is the only way you will ever guarantee your own happiness.

Although there was not a microscopic part of my being that wanted to go and do this job, I weighed my options and knew I needed to do something different to move forward. I would not say our relationship ended, but at this point Robert and I parted ways to do what we each had to do.

EARNING MY POSITION

I received my promotion letter in August 1986. By now, my father understood that traveling was becoming a bit cumbersome and that it was important to be mindful of the type and *location* of my assignments. Despite his commitment to the business, as my father, he did want me to be happy. He understood what was fair to me and what was not, so he offered me an assignment with Mars department stores.

Located in Taunton, Massachusetts, Mars was in an old mill town. It was another dim speck on the US map, but it wasn't exactly in the middle of nowhere.

The senior auditor on this assignment was Jim Brown, a man who'd worked with CCA for many years. With so much work to be completed, they decided to divide the audit into two pieces. Jim performed the accounts payable audit, and I worked on the freight audit.

The divide sounds even enough—that is, until you consider where these tasks placed us. Dearest Jim was cozied up behind a desk in the middle of the air-conditioned accounts payable department. I, on the other hand, was stationed in a closet where all the freight bills were stored, with no air-conditioning, no desk, and a whole lot of dust.

Stuck in a hot storage room with only windows in the dead of summer, I still managed to uncover more money than Jim. This young, inexperienced, ill-positioned auditor—the boss's brat, if you will—didn't let my circumstances get the best of my performance.

Since I was the junior auditor on the assignment, Jim would be better compensated on our distribution. He found about $18,000, and I recovered around $93,000. Because of this, Jim thought it fair to initiate a fifty-fifty auditor split of commissions, confirming the fact that I'd duly earned the respect of my position, at least with Jim.

Taunton's proximity to Cape Cod did present a positive for this audit. Not only was I close to our new family home, in the *summer*, I wasn't far from my dear college roommate Frances, who was now working in nearby Boston. For the first time in a while, my social life had regained a pulse.

THE GLAMOROUS LIFE OF A FIELD AUDITOR

Next up, in the fall of 1986, I moved on to the Ames audit. This was one of the first times I was allowed to juggle more than one account at once. Ames basically claimed the next several years of my career. I was not complaining much, at least not at first. Ames was proving to be one of the most successful audits that I, at the age of twenty-four, had yet worked on. With $130,000 in commissions headed my way, I was loving the business even more.

But the rewards of the job were not without hard, sometimes grimy work.

Our first specialty assignment was with Staples, in Framingham, Massachusetts, in an old New England warehouse accented with blown-out windows and a questionable freight elevator. It was a little creepy, to be honest.

Staples took our promise to do all the work as literally as any client ever has. They pointed their finger toward the warehouse, which was clearly just a place where employees did pickups or drop-offs of file storage boxes. Nobody was working out of that place except us. That dusty, derelict old building became our headquarters for the next several months.

Talk about being humble.

For the same reasons that had me living out of a trailer in Ocala, we would not rent office space during an audit. The idea was to keep our costs as low as humanly possible. Instead of fancy setups, we opted for what we knew and dusted off those classic brown folding tables and chairs and set up shop.

Ready though I was to look beyond our setting and get to work, my soul almost left my body one day when I was frightened by a possum-sized rat that sauntered across the floor.

Hazards of the job, I guess. Or perhaps it was just another change we had to learn to accept.

Post the October 1987 stock market crash, when the Dow lost 22.6 percent of its value in one day, some of our accounts were moving toward bankruptcy or Chapter 11, including Ames, which ate away at my pending earnings. We started to recognize some pain points in our payment structure, which didn't allow for progress payments for assignments that went on for multiple months. This meant that our fees could fall victim to a bankruptcy filing, leaving us without payment for work already completed. The $130,000 in commissions from Ames I mentioned at the beginning of this section? Poof. I ended up with just pennies on the dollar.

The silver lining of this was that CCA modified its payment terms going forward to be timelier, avoiding what I experienced as a result of a bankruptcy. And despite bumps in the road, somehow CCA continued to prosper.

Even though there was much to celebrate during this time, those victories could not save us from the devastating turn of events that suddenly flipped our lives upside down. Sometimes change can sneak up on you so swiftly there isn't enough time to anticipate the impact it can have on your business and your life. The next chapter of our story taught us lessons that will remain with our family forever.

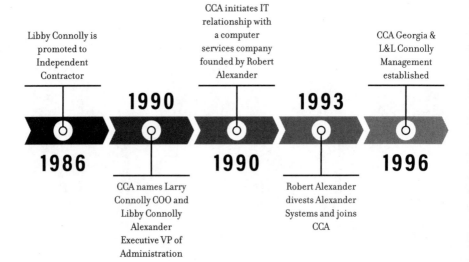

Libby Connolly is promoted to Independent Contractor

CCA initiates IT relationship with a computer services company founded by Robert Alexander

CCA Georgia & L&L Connolly Management established

1990

1993

1986

1990

1996

CCA names Larry Connolly COO and Libby Connolly Alexander Executive VP of Administration

Robert Alexander divests Alexander Systems and joins CCA

CHAPTER 4

Leadership Transition

Passing the Baton

*No one gave us an instruction manual on
how to run and grow a business.*

—Libby Connolly Alexander

The late summer of 1986 marked a transformative moment for me. My career was steadily advancing. Judging by my year-end review, it was clear I could handle myself in the field. Positive feedback from my father and the senior CCA staff I worked for led to my officially signing on as an independent contractor. No longer limited by my administrative and audit assistant roles,

I finally hit my stride. I was confident, even though I had a lot to learn. My assigned audits were flourishing nicely, and the company was recognizing my contributions. Not to mention, all my work was earning me a lot of money.

I was enjoying the moment. Professionally, life was treating me well. My family was going through a few positive changes too. My parents had decided to sell our family home in Rye, then moved to North Falmouth, Cape Cod. Whisked away by dreams of retirement, they felt moving back to Massachusetts meant they could be closer to old friends and the people they loved.

Sarcastically, my mother accused my father of buying a dock. The house they purchased was in a new waterfront development, and it did, in fact, have a protected deep-water dock, a rare find on Buzzards Bay. While the house was brand new and beautiful, my mother knew it was the dock that had caught my father's attention. With a home so close to the water, my parents could keep *Tranquility*, their Pearson 10M sailboat, at the house. Later, *Tranquility* was sold and replaced with *Duet*, my father's precious forty-two-foot trawler that he enjoyed for many years.

Living on the Cape was a dream come true for my parents. Settled into their new space, the plan was for them to spend many tranquil years together. All my father needed was the right time to step away from the business, so he could retire and enjoy the life he'd created for the two of them.

Their move from New York to Massachusetts forced me to make a few changes as well. Work already required full-time travel, but I still needed a place to hang my hat. After surveying my options, Darien, Connecticut, seemed like the most promising place to treat as my home base. Robert and three other good friends from college days were working in the area and renting a house at 149 Nearwater

Lane, just a block from the beach. Like my parents, I longed to be closer to the people I loved, and this little arrangement seemed like the perfect opportunity.

Appreciating its original character and charm, I moved into the classic old New England farmhouse. Robert and I had separate rooms, but being so close rekindled our relationship, and before long, we started dating again.

Our love was about the only warm thing in that house. Its traditional design had very little insulation. In fact, you could see straight through the wide-plank pinewood floors into the basement!

Winters in Connecticut are unforgiving, so you can only imagine how cold it got inside. Freezing our tails off, we used to call the little farmhouse "Ice Station Zebra," a reference to the film of the same name that takes place in the Arctic. But the five of us turned that space into a home. There were three guys downstairs, and me and another girlfriend in the rooms on the upper level. We were a group of hopeful twentysomethings doing our best to figure out where we belonged in this crazy world.

We all liked to have fun. And we definitely did. My life was finally beginning to be balanced in a way that I'd hoped for.

It seemed as if the fruits of my father's planning were already ripening. We were all happy, and the business was growing. At this stage in our story, the calculated risks my father had taken were paying off.

Nevertheless, considering all the time I invested in my assignments, I rarely had any left for myself. Mars and Ames department stores were my primary accounts at the time, which meant I was usually on the road traveling northbound. Ames was headquartered in Rocky Hill, Connecticut, just outside of Hartford, and Mars was located in Taunton, Massachusetts, not too far from Boston. I could commute to Rocky Hill, but when I was working at Mars, I had to split my time. I went from bumming a couch in Boston from my college roommate Frances to a bed at my parents' new house on Cape Cod.

It was an adjustment but welcomed still. The time I spent with my family and friends was night and day in comparison to the way I'd been living for the previous year buried in Bentonville and isolated in Ocala.

Everything seemed so perfect. Maybe *too* perfect for the laws of polarity. That's when tragedy hit.

AN IMPOSSIBLE, HEARTBREAKING DILEMMA

One October morning, my mother woke up feeling less than her usual self. She had turned sixty but was in incredible shape. Always active and on the go, she never let a day go by without finding time to spend a few hours on the tennis court. With that said, none of us were prepared for what was about to occur.

Doctors discovered my mother was suffering from an undiagnosed heart condition that led to the failure of her mitral valve. What began as a routine day quickly turned into admission to the New England Deaconess Hospital. She needed surgery immediately. Time was of the essence.

Word of her condition left us full of unanswered questions. We all wanted to know how something like this could happen so suddenly. At the same time, we were comforted in knowing that she was in good hands. The head of the hospital happened to be one of my parents' closest friends. He assured us that he would personally oversee her care.

My mother spent several days in Deaconess before the surgery, but she remained in good spirits the entire time. Geographically, my father and I were closer than anyone else, so we became her on-the-ground support team. Finding out she was ill was very unsettling. At the same time, I was on the road working hard as a newly minted independent contractor and juggling a lot on my plate.

Camping out with Frances in Boston made things a little easier. My father drove back and forth from the Cape to be at my mother's bedside during the day. I spent my working hours in Taunton, then traveled to the hospital at night to relieve him. This trade-off became our routine. This way, my mother never felt like she was alone. Calls and flowers came in from my siblings, relatives, and many of her friends. She was showered with love and affection, which she adored.

On the day of the surgery, my father and I were both by her side. Everything at the hospital felt routine. She was taken into the operating room, and after several hours, we received word of a successful procedure.

Hospital officials invited us to join her in the recovery room one at a time. My father was the first to enter. It did not take long for us to realize that something was wrong, terribly wrong.

The surgery itself had been uneventful, but my mother had had two severe strokes during recovery. Her brain was swelling, she was becoming less and less responsive, and the doctors' optimism quickly dissolved into a grim articulation of *options*. The situation rapidly collapsed, and in a moment's notice, things were no longer as simple as alternating between bedside visits.

My father decided it was time to call my siblings.

Larry arrived from New York the next afternoon. Then Carol from North Carolina and Jim from Chicago. The five of us gathered at the same place where our trusted family friend first told us everything would be just fine. Optimism shifted into the need for answers.

It was time to have a conversation that no family should ever have to have.

My parents' friend, the head of the hospital, tried to console us in our time of need. He had the difficult task of explaining my mother's deteriorating condition and ran us through the possibilities. As I listened to his suggestions, each option sounded more devastating than the last.

Without intervention, the swelling in my mother's brain would become fatal. Decompression surgery was something to consider, but it presented its own risks. No one could predict how impaired my mother would be in the aftermath. Our next meeting was with the hospital's head brain surgeon. Extremely competent and sure, he reiterated the opinions we'd already heard, but with the confidence only a brain surgeon could have. Regardless of what we decided, there were no guarantees. Time was of the essence. We needed to make a decision.

My father was heartbroken. All of us were, but his pain was piercing. He knew that the strokes and the surgery would leave my mother in such a terrible state that no matter what we did, her life, *their* life, would never be the same. With the clock ticking, we sat down as a family to figure out what would be in my mother's best interest.

I must say, I sincerely believe my father wanted to let her go, but he was also afraid of being judged for not trying to save her. My oldest brother, Jim, was emotional and felt very strongly about moving forward with the surgery. One by one, all of my mother's children offered their opinion. All except one.

The voice inside my mind was screaming to be recognized, but I refused to concede to its demands. I never spoke up. I never said anything. No one in that room wanted to vote against saving our mother's life, including me.

Whenever I think back on that time, I often question why I struggled to say what was in my heart. I am the youngest of my mother's children, with considerable gaps between me and my older siblings. I supposed that was one contributing factor. When my brother Jim, who was eleven years my senior, spoke up, I stayed quiet. I wish I hadn't.

My inner voice told me that Mom would never accept the idea of being handicapped, not just physically, but emotionally. But despite what I felt she would have preferred, I refused to raise objection. So moving forward with the surgery became a unanimous family decision.

I behaved like a coward. I could not muster up the strength to find my voice. We all have at least one memory that makes us utter that famous line, "I wish I could turn back the hands of time." This was mine.

November 1986 marked a period in my mother's life when she lost not only her health but her dignity. She lived for another five years and four months. For the rest of her days, she was bound to a wheelchair. She had no mobility in either of her legs, her left arm, or most of her right arm as well. To make matters worse, between the strokes and the surgeries, her speech was severely impaired.

All the while, she remained mentally cognizant about everything that was happening. This meant she was awfully aware of the way life had left her paralyzed, and for her, it was a living hell.

After the surgery, she required full-time care. She went from being active and thriving to being unable to do anything for herself. Fortunately, Robert was pretty handy and incredibly gracious. He volunteered to build a ramp extension for the home on the Cape, so my mother could access it by wheelchair. As much as we appreciated his gesture, that was probably the beginning and end of my mother's comfort.

PUTTING THE "FAMILY" IN FAMILY BUSINESS

Dealing with such a monumental tragedy in my twenties was something I did not know I had the strength to handle. I always regretted having my time with my mother cut short so soon, but coping with her illness taught me things I would one day pass on to my peers. There's never a textbook solution to losing a parent, but I am now able to console my friends through lessons learned from experience.

Still, that does not cancel how painful it was to watch my mother suffer, just when our family started to expand. She was unhappy about not having any grandchildren, even before she fell ill. Having the chance to renew her sense of purpose with new bundles of joy to play with is all any matronly empty nester really wants. At the time of her illness, grandchildren weren't yet part of the equation. Her youngest children were not married, and although the oldest were, babies were delayed.

In the years to come, our family dynamic evolved. My mother's condition weighed on her and my father even more, and she was eventually transferred to a long-term care facility in St. Petersburg, Florida, to receive the care she needed. The move drove her away from her family, friends, and the beautiful home in which she and her husband were supposed to retire. Out of options, we did our best to make the transition as tolerable as possible, which meant many weekend trips to Florida to help my father with her care.

In March 1988, Larry married his wife, Leigh. And by 1990, my relationship with Robert was headed to the altar as well. We wed in St. Petersburg, just so my mother could attend the ceremony. We did not realize it back then, but our two relationships shared many similarities. Robert and I had our first date on New Year's Eve. Coincidentally, Larry and his wife also met at a New Year's Eve celebration. We exchanged vows within a short time of one another, and we both had our first children only a few years apart.

Our extended family was growing as well. By 1990 my brother Jim and his wife Nancy had their first two children, Jac and Nick Connolly, and my sister, Carol and her husband Branson had their two children, Elizabeth and Connor Bruce. Larry and Leigh's firstborn, Jay, was on the way, followed soon thereafter by a daughter, Greer. But it was still a bittersweet time.

My mother was not mobile, and her speech was not very strong, but she could see and understand everything that was going on. All of her children were finally married, and her wish of becoming a grandmother was finally realized, but she could only look on in longing, knowing that she was not strong enough to hold her grandbabies in her arms. It was emotional torture.

That wasn't the only change that rocked our family to the core.

Whether my mother knew or not, I will never know, but around the same time, my father took up a relationship with another woman. A woman whom he would later marry. It was completely unexpected and unforeseen, but now that I've had time to process the situation, I can see why it had to happen.

My father was in the later years of his life, and watching my mother's health fail and her will be broken took a toll on him. He didn't want to spend the last of his days wallowing in regret or despair. He wanted to be happy. His new relationship gave him the opportunity to see life through a different lens. We may not have recognized it at the time, but that was one of the first things Jim Connolly did that was strictly for him.

I have to say, even with him pursuing a new take on love and life, he always put my mother first. He was incredibly respectful and, as far as I know, kept his new relationship completely separate from my mother's affairs.

So much changed within our family in the five years after she fell ill. Fortunately, I can say that I had the pleasure of announcing my pregnancy with my firstborn, Aaron, before my mother passed away in January 1992. Between her death and my giving birth six months later, there was a lot for me to process. I had to fulfill many roles, as a wife, a mother, a daughter, and a critical member of the management of a company that was demanding much of my attention.

Evaluating his remaining life, the future with his soon-to-be wife, and the trajectory the company had taken, my father decided it was time to prepare for his retirement.

Seeing the circumstances through his eyes, I can understand why he felt it was time to shift the company in a new direction. He was sixty-nine years old at the time. He was not the same enterprising young man that had once taken the retail world by storm. Many of his peers had already retired by sixty, yet he still sat at the head of the table of a fast-track business that needed to respond to pressing industry concerns.

And we need to consider his mind-set. After watching his wife cling to life in an institution for a year, he couldn't tolerate it any longer. Ignoring his age, he volunteered to oversee her care full-time. Caring for her required a lot more than anyone could've imagined. By the time we reached 1990, my father was beginning to check out from the business. By 1991, he was ready to move on[11].

Life, stress, and strain forced him into autopilot for a while, but since we had such a sound business model, CCA still remained afloat.

Evaluating his life and his lineage, I think he felt it was time to start celebrating, time to start focusing on himself. Both of his parents passed of heart disease his mother at fifty-one, his father at

---

11   James A. Connolly, Beginning-of-New-Decade Report. January 1, 1991.

sixty-one and his youngest brother at fifty-four. At sixty-nine, his life was like an accomplishment in itself.

Things were changing all around him. He'd found someone who enjoyed all the things he loved. They played tennis together and sat around the piano as she played, and he sang all the old war ditties he enjoyed. Even with all the newness she brought into his life, he knew he couldn't just walk away from the business.

Transferring leadership over to Larry and me was a calculated risk he was willing to take, one that allowed him to honor his happiness without abandoning everything he'd created. He was a new grandparent too. He wanted to enjoy the fullness of his life as he walked into a new chapter. You saw a glimpse of his enjoyment in the story shared about his seventy-fifth birthday party in the opening of this memoir. He wanted to continue that momentum without sacrificing the future of the business.

The principals were breathing down his back because, with all his distractions, my father was no longer beating the pavement in search of new clientele, and the business was facing additional headwinds due to "the rash of mergers, acquisitions, consolidations, restructurings, bankruptcies, highly intensified competition, and price cutting."[12] CCA was coasting along, but if we didn't continue to work toward forward progression, we would be passed by the competition.

By January 1991, we were four years into my mother's tragedy, and things had not improved. Her care was pulling my father further and further from the duties of the business, leaving a void that Larry and I were only partially filling. My father knew he didn't have the bandwidth to lead the company, take care of my mother, and spend time with his new love. Therefore, it was announced that Larry would be promoted to chief operating officer, and I became the executive VP

---

12   Ibid.

of administration. As a part of the agreement, my father continued to serve as executive chairman.

> "The climate for our business promises to continue to be difficult and challenging into the foreseeable future. This places a high premium on having an operating management that is young, energetic, and highly motivated … "

> **—James A. Connolly**
> Beginning-of-New-Decade Report
> January 1, 1991

A year later, I was starting a family, my father's involvement had been largely reduced, and Robert was becoming more important to the business. Larry was focusing on sales, and it was working. The business was starting to grow again, we needed to reinvest, and compensation needed to be addressed. In a memorandum of understanding from a meeting with Larry and my father in December 1992, we addressed the basis for future salary distributions. Through this meeting, my father acknowledged the fact that, after 1991, he was no longer active in the management of the company, and because of that, his previous compensation, including amounts paid to him to pass through to his estate, could no longer be rationalized. He also addressed the fact that previous attempts to sell the business determined that it had no value, which made the inheritance value of CCA "virtually nil," so it would not be fair to burden Larry and me with estate obligations.

By this time, the company was two years into our relationship with Alexander Systems, a computer consulting and services company my husband, Robert, founded. Acting initially as an advisor, Robert was in charge of helping us conceive and lay the foundation for a technology strategy that would sustain CCA in light of several industry changes.

In 1992, both PRG and Howard Schultz, our two largest competitors, announced the establishment of new data centers. Standing firm in my father's belief that a little competitive paranoia was healthy for your business, we paid close attention to the industry, recognizing areas we needed to master long before our competition took over that sector. In this case, technology was the new wave. Offering sound advice and demonstrating know-how, Robert soon became one of the business's most trusted resources. Whenever he told us to do something, we essentially nodded in agreement. Eventually, it was clear that we needed his undivided knowledge and expertise if we were going to compete in an environment where having technology capability was fast becoming a differentiator.

Standing firm in my father's belief that a little competitive paranoia was healthy for your business, we paid close attention to the industry, recognizing areas we needed to master long before our competition took over that sector.

My father, Larry, and I had a meeting to discuss making a proposition to Robert to convince him to sell Alexander Systems and join CCA full time:

```
We in CCA are all convinced that it will be
impossible to continue to be a major player
in paid bills auditing in the future unless
we continue to possess the cutting-edge EDP
analyzing and processing capabilities we
```

have thus far developed. In the last two
or three years, Robert Alexander has played
a major role in designing and processing
systems for CA to process clients' paid
media tape files to facilitate post audits.

John Connolly then reported that he has
reason to believe that Robert Alexander
would be receptive to an appropriate offer
to close out his own successful business and
join and join the company … on a full-time
basis.

—December 1992 Minutes, Special Meeting of
the Board of Directors

From that point on, Robert, Larry, and I became a dynamic trio.
The business was all consuming, but the three of us were all in.

In the same meeting that discussed the value Robert brought to
the company, there were shared a few classically sexist suggestions
about my future performance. No matter the time or the era, there
will always be a few unsettling stigmas about women lingering in the
business realm. I was scheduled to give birth any day, and it was subtly implied that Robert could "pick up the slack" while I was "distracted by domestic matters." In spite of the assumptions made about my maternal capabilities, I was determined to prove that I could continue to be as influential

There was this assumption that I would become "domesticated" by motherhood. As if having a baby weakens a woman's resolve. If anything, my children forced me to work harder than ever.

and involved with our business as I was before getting pregnant. I gave birth, and within two weeks, I was back at work.

I never missed a beat. Quite frankly, I do not know why anyone would have expected anything different. I never declared that I wanted to stay at home, but there was this assumption that I would become "domesticated" by motherhood. As if having a baby weakens a woman's resolve. If anything, my children forced me to work harder than ever. My mother's words always echoed in the back of my mind, and when she passed, I was committed to making her proud. She always told me to make sure that I was financially independent, and I wasn't going to let her down.

This pattern continued with each child: two weeks after each delivery, I was back on the job.

People always ask me, "How'd you do it? How did you manage to have four kids in five years and continue to be so involved in your business?" The answer is simple: it was my only option.

We were a small business without keyman backup, and we didn't have maternity or paternity leave policies. Out of necessity, from day one, I set myself up to be a successful working mother. I was committed to my family, and the company was our sole livelihood. I knew that torturing myself with the thought of staying home would be nothing more than a distraction. Instead, I took a page from my father's book and calculated a way to keep working.

I used the resources I had available to create a caring and stable environment at home. Robert and I had created such an amazing support system, I knew my children were always in great hands. Going back to work was not up for discussion. We were not making enough money for me to stay at home. I had to work. I had to help provide for my family.

In the same respect, another question I get all the time is

why—"Why did your father decide to transfer leadership of the business over to you and Larry?"

Of course there were principals who were far more experienced than us, at least in retail years, but that option never played out. So my answer is, we were being groomed for our positions long before we formally assumed the role. My father's previous attempts at selling the business were unsuccessful, and very little had changed within the business since then. Our topline was contracting, the competitive landscape with clients like Walmart was becoming more challenging, and rates were declining right before our eyes. Investing in us was his best option for generating long-term returns from the business. There was always a method to Jim Connolly's madness. I believe he knew exactly what he was doing when he shuffled us off into the field to work on client engagements in addition to having Larry develop direct relationships with all of CCA's principals.

We were being trained to be leaders and, with the guidance and wisdom we'd gained from watching our father for our entire lives, he trusted that we'd be able to make decisions modeled after his own leadership style in the best interest of the business.

"Larry and Libby Connolly are deeply steeped in the principles which have enabled CCA to be … successful … They, together with Robert Alexander, bring to CCA an abundance of youth, strength, enthusiasm, and high motivation, as well as much expertise in computer-based auditing as anyone currently practicing—at a point in time when these qualities are foremost among those most needed for success."

—James A. Connolly, Beginning-of-New-Decade
Report, January 1, 1991

We invested a lot of sweat equity into CCA, and with Robert's added technology capability, we proved that we were more than capable of continuing its success.

For me personally, that meant making sacrifices and planning my moves in advance. It meant placing the business's needs first and modeling my life around that. I had to assemble a trustworthy and reliable support system to help me with my children. My mother-in-law was always there when we needed her, and Robert and I were fortunate enough to find a wonderful person, Brenda Bagley, who cared for our children and stayed with our family for twenty years. She was only the second childcare provider that we ever hired. The first, Alison Patnick, a.k.a. Nanny, worked at our home for two years before coming to join us at the Stamford office as our first administrative assistant.

When I say we put the "family" in family business, everything we did was an example of that.

Personal connections served us in more ways than one. When you hire people you trust, be it handing over your business to the care of your two youngest children or entrusting your newborns to another's care, healthy long-term relationships are critical. It was these types of relationships that allowed CCA to grow to its fullest potential.

RESPONDING TO INDUSTRY DEMANDS

For the first time ever, CCA was feeling the weight of industry competition. Our "healthy competitive paranoia" was now bordering on concern as clients took advantage of the rate war sparked by a growing number of competitors offering lower fees. Before Larry and I were inducted into our new roles, the company's principals gathered with my father in Chicago for their first meeting in January 1988. "Rate compression" was the topic of the hour. They needed to discuss the possibility of reducing our own rates and, if so, under what circumstances. Until that point, the formula was pretty standard. Primary rates were around 45 percent and secondary rates 50 percent. The days of those high rates were clearly numbered!

Movement in the market nationally had everyone wondering if it was time to concede on rates. Fresh in everyone's mind was that we had just lost the Walmart account to a competitor because we were unwilling to lower our rate. My father and his principals sat down to contemplate a consistent strategy outlining how CCA would approach the rate war.[13]

The eponymous Howard Schultz company, one of the industry's pioneering giants, had spent the last few decades securing the majority of the US grocery market while at the same time expanding into international territories. After establishing a foundation in Canada, the UK, Ireland, and Europe, the company was on track to box out any sort of competition.

Domestically, things were shifting as well. In 1989, John M. Cook resigned from his position as the chief financial officer at Caldor Stores to broker a deal to become the COO of Roy Greene and Associates, the small Atlanta-based recovery auditing firm he'd once hired to service his company.[14] His primary focus was to transform the processes used to complete an audit, as he believed that software could make the industry much more efficient. Shortly thereafter,

---

13   Managers' Meeting Agenda, "What kind of business do we want to run, anyway?" Chicago, January 1988.

14   Michael Smeriglio III, CPA, PRG-Schultz International Inc. company profile.

Cook went on to buy the business outright, partnering with John M. Toma, a former associate from Caldor. Together, they founded the Profit Recovery Group (PRG) in 1990. In the coming years, PRG support staff was tasked with "scouring the country—and, increasingly, Europe and Asia as well—in a continuing search to identify likely acquisition targets, in accordance with a complicated model ... of what sort of acquisition would suit PRG's business interests best."[15]

The company went through a complete rebranding. This was a big deal in our industry, and John Cook spared no opportunity to discuss his future plans. According to him, it was time to proceed with a "new vision," one that shifted the recovery audit business into a medium that regularly leveraged technology.

His strategy was simple: buy up the competition.

The industry was fragmented and ripe for consolidating all the mom-and-pops, assuming that less competition would help stabilize rates and result in more consistent profits. Many of the companies who sold saw PRG as a compelling exit strategy. Technology capabilities were becoming a ticket to entry in the recovery audit industry, requiring capital investment as well as an increase in sales and marketing muscle. By the late '90s, PRG was becoming such a competitive force, we also thought we should explore an exit strategy with PRG. They were big, getting bigger, and were much more sophisticated operationally. They had resources we didn't, and in order to compete, we were going to have to raise our own bar and figure out how to "grow or die."[16]

---

15   The Profit Recovery Group, *Case A: Upping the Pace in Audit Recovery*. Nijenrode University Press.

16   In an interview with Larry Connolly in preparation for this book, he described the fierce market and competitive challenges Connolly faced in the 1990s after the leadership transition occurred, and the primary strategy for Connolly was "we

ISSUES OF FAIRNESS

Competition was heating up, and client fee rates were continuing to compress. Both PRG and Schultz were making announcements about the creation of new data centers and their focus on investing in technology. We knew we needed to respond in kind.

At the time, Larry and I were handling some of CCA's administrative matters, but most of our schedule was still committed to working client engagements, and much of our income was still earned from our audit commissions.

One by one, my father made sure each of the principals were aware of his intention to promote Larry and me to our new leadership positions. Since we had already developed relationships with most of the founding principals, it was not very difficult for them to accept the change in authority. That's why we were taken aback when we first learned of the plans being undertaken by one of our father's first principals—and dear friend—Marty Goldman. The same man who was once one of my father's most trusted advisors took us all by surprise when he threatened to leave the company and take his book of business, *CCA's* book of business, with him.

Some of the original principals were dynamic salesmen who had their own deep industry contacts and could secure and manage their own accounts. Others needed my father to step in as "the closer" to help them gain new clients. Marty was one of the latter.

By the time Marty joined the company in 1983, my father already had a substantial client base established in the Northeast, which is what he agreed to assign to Marty. My father's influence kept Marty as the head of lucrative accounts that totaled about 38 percent of CCA's business. Sometime shortly after the 1988 princi-

---

either had to grow or be prepared to die." Die meant conceding to the competition and selling out to PRG who, at the time, was consolidating the industry.

pals' meeting in Chicago, Marty learned that the fee-sharing arrangements between CCA and its principals varied. He discovered that Dan Shaps, principal of the Midwest region, was receiving a higher percentage on his audits than he was. Marty convinced himself that managing client relationships and overseeing the independent contractors on his clients meant he was running his own company. Abandoning all logic or long-term concern, Marty succumbed to an emotionally charged response to something he only partially understood.

What Marty did not realize was that Dan's accounts were paid as such because Dan took the lead in sourcing, securing, staffing, and retaining each one. In Marty's case, my father laid all the groundwork for him. Marty used the "absentee owner" clause as a defense, claiming that whatever my father did for him in the beginning was no longer relevant. It's amazing how much a misunderstanding can change the fabric of what was once a fruitful union.

Since the day Marty started working for Connolly, he and my father would talk on the telephone every Saturday for hours on end. Very suddenly, the calls stopped, and eventually, they were barely communicating. Maybe if they'd met in person, things would've turned out differently. Unfortunately, they never found common ground, so my father and his former friend chose to settle their dispute a different way.

Envelopes addressed to my father would come in the mail, and he'd then sit down with Larry and me to get our opinion. We'd infer what we assumed Marty meant in his messages, and then my father would dictate his response. Back and forth, Larry and I would chime in to suggest how Marty might receive our father's words. After a few revisions, my father would put his reply in the mail. This discussion went on for a while, before Marty went too far, pushing my father to the point where he was finished with "talking."

The last offense that ended all further negotiation was when Marty sent a letter saying something like, "If you don't give me more favorable terms, I'm going to have to do what's best for me, my clients, and my auditors."

It was clear that we were at an impasse, so my father advised us to terminate CCA's relationship with Marty. He wanted to avoid the risk of Marty leading other principals down the same path of independence. If the rest of the principals followed Marty's lead, that would have been the undoing of CCA. The necessary response was obvious, but we still wanted to handle the separation delicately.

To avoid disruption and client relationship risk, my father advised a plan for others to take over his accounts. CCA had qualified individuals within its talent pool to promote from within who, when approached by Larry about the opportunity for advancement, were more than happy to take on the accounts Marty was managing.

It was a classic case of overplaying one's hand, and what's even more ironic is the fact that Marty was expecting loyalty from his clients and the independent contractors he managed when he clearly had no sense of it himself. Realistically speaking, big companies are accustomed to turnover; they see it every day. His clients were more concerned with the job getting done than with CCA's internal affairs. As it turned out, it was not hard to explain his replacements.

Eventually, my father picked up the phone to tell his old friend he regretted the way things ended. The conversation closed with him telling Marty it was best if they went separate ways. Marty hung up and told his wife, Bunny, "I think I just got fired," but that's not exactly what happened.

Marty really wasn't prepared to go out on his own and start competing against Connolly, PRG, Schultz, and all the others. Like my father, he too was at retirement age. Instead, Marty was given an offer that allowed him to plan for his retirement and leave the business he'd invested many years into with dignity. He was able to retain the few accounts he had independently secured, and the fee sharing was adjusted to be consistent. This gave Marty the option to stay with CCA, which he did for several years after the disagreement.

The account transfer and settlement process with Marty gave us a blueprint for how to handle subsequent principal retirements, some forced, some not. Competition in the marketplace was heating up, and there was no time for complacency. Larry made it his mission to visit, one by one, each of the other principals throughout each year. One by one, he had those difficult planning conversations with each of them. Everyone knew how we'd severed ties with Marty, and from then on, we were not met with much resistance.

With the threat extinguished, Larry proved his ability to lead the company with a firm yet compassionate hand. Marty was allowed enough time to transition out of his assignments; the entire situation was orderly and respectful. We even maintained a healthy professional relationship with his son, Sam, after Marty left. Having my father mentor us through that challenging time helped us get past the situation with little upset.

Either way, I am glad that we chose to let long-term relationships prevail over the dismay. That is what CCA was all about. Decisions like this were perfectly aligned with my father's philosophy around fairness and it showed the rest of the team that CCA without Jim Connolly would remain fair as well. CCA was more than profit margins and percentages. We were people driven by passion

CCA was more than profit margins and percentages. We were people driven by passion and purpose, but more importantly, we lived our beliefs through our business as well.

and purpose, but more importantly, we lived our beliefs through our business as well.

AN OFFICIAL CHANGE

Continued competition from Schultz and PRG meant it was time for us to prioritize our "grow or die" strategy to meet the industry's new technological demand. Now that my father was confident in our ability to lead the company, there was one more official move to make.

In 1996, PRG's going public instigated an estate crisis for my father. For the first time, there was a valuation benchmark for the business. Since he still retained the vast majority of CCA's ownership at the time, upon his death, CCA would be part of his entire estate and taxed for its value. Our only option would have been to sell the business to come up with the cash to pay the estate tax.

To avoid this issue, we devised a plan. We established a new company in Georgia called Connolly Consulting Associates, with ownership split equally between Larry's family and mine. Next, we established L&L Connolly Associates, based in Connecticut, which was owned equally between Larry and me. With this move, Larry's family and mine each held fifty percent of the company's shares. Although this seemed to us to be a major shift, for our clients and ICs it was uneventful, they were working with the same people—the same company.

As the new leaders and owners of CCA, Larry and I agreed on our first order of business: growth and expansion. We were fast approaching the day of the "new Connolly." The leadership transition was solidified, our client relationships were intact and the ownership structure reorganized, new business was being secured, and our top line was growing once again. The competition thought we were small and unsophisticated, but CCA would soon prove that we could become a market leader. Although the details were still unclear, we were quickly beginning to understand that technology would be the game changer that would reshape our industry and CCA's trajectory forever.

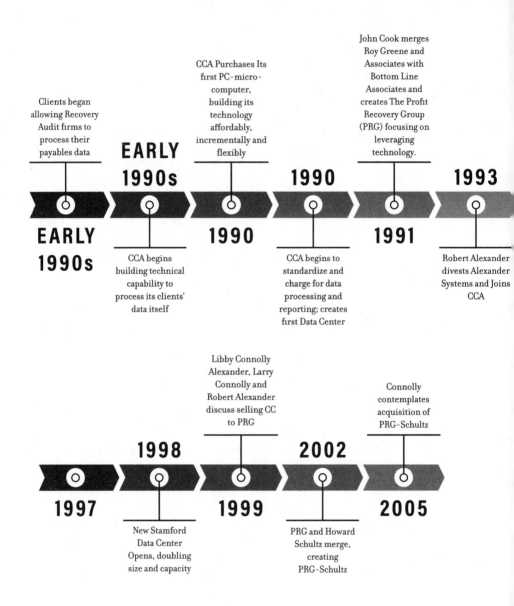

Clients began allowing Recovery Audit firms to process their payables data

EARLY 1990s

CCA Purchases Its first PC-micro-computer, building its technology affordably, incrementally and flexibly

1990

John Cook merges Roy Greene and Associates with Bottom Line Associates and creates The Profit Recovery Group (PRG) focusing on leveraging technology.

1993

EARLY 1990s

CCA begins building technical capability to process its clients' data itself

1990

CCA begins to standardize and charge for data processing and reporting; creates first Data Center

1991

Robert Alexander divests Alexander Systems and Joins CCA

Libby Connolly Alexander, Larry Connolly and Robert Alexander discuss selling CC to PRG

1998

2002

Connolly contemplates acquisition of PRG-Schultz

1997

1999

2005

New Stamford Data Center Opens, doubling size and capacity

PRG and Howard Schultz merge, creating PRG-Schultz

CHAPTER 5

Growth

Developing an Evolving Strategy

I've never been a big gambler, and I don't believe in making big bets. If you have a big idea, start small, prove the concept, and figure it out. I call that "cracking the code."

—Libby Connolly Alexander

D espite the tragedies, challenges, and changes that followed into the early '90s, we knew we could withstand the industry's shift by putting all our attention into building one main area of our business. For us, growth meant conservative expansion, starting with technology. We were more than willing to make investments in the things necessary to keep us relevant in the marketplace, but we would do so conservatively, following our philosophy of taking a calculated risk and not making big, expensive bets.

For us, growth meant conservative expansion, starting with technology.

Because of PRG's massive footprint of clients and infrastructure, they opted to invest in large-scale mainframes, assuming a costly and complex tech strategy. CCA chose to travel down a different road and only focused on doing what we could with the technology we could afford. We had no clue at the time that the personal computer path would eventually become our secret weapon.

After reading the press releases and listening to the way the market gushed over John Cook's new vision for PRG, it was obvious that we needed to figure out our own way to leverage technology. Without the budget or the resources to compete with the heavy-weights, we had to get creative with our delivery.

The "new Connolly" needed to make some adjustments, and technology was step one of creating our new identity. Evolution and investments came in incremental stages. We didn't have a lot of excess capital, certainly not the type of capital our larger competitors had, and therefore we only added resources in a very deliberate and on an as-needed basis. Living within your means was a core philosophy we adhered to, whether it was equipment, our salaries, the cars we drove or even the houses we lived in, and we were determined to grow without taking on debt. Our business was built one client at a time, and we took the same incremental approach with adapting to technology.

We didn't believe in making big, risky bets, thus minimizing the impact of potential losses. When it came to doing something new, we would try it out, see how it worked, then resource accordingly. The "grow or die" strategy eventually paved the way for one of our first major trials. We decided to contract some help from an extremely talented, tech-savvy young man, who just happened to be my husband.

> *We didn't believe in making big, risky bets, thus minimizing the impact of potential losses.*

HOW WE CHANGED THE GAME WITH
THE PERSONAL COMPUTER

When PRG went on record about their full-fledged focus on technology, we knew we had to respond. At the time, Robert was successfully managing his own computer consulting business, Alexander Systems, out of Stamford, Connecticut, and it only made sense to lean on him for expertise we didn't have.

Following his instruction, CCA bought our first PC in 1990, beginning what would become a long-term commitment to a PC technology strategy. Little did we know at the time that this strategy would become a key competitive differentiator. He also helped us establish how the business would distribute the costs of the new technology across audits, outlined in a "computer policy" that was shared with the principals and later revised as our investments in technology increased over time. Thankfully, Robert was there to be our backbone through everything we were trying to develop, not simply the technology itself but also the resulting impact it had on so many aspects of our business.

Investing in the microcomputer—the moniker given to PCs in the early 1990s to distinguish them from mainframes and the emerging minicomputers—was not a fly-by decision. It was a big—but calculated—risk for us back then, allowing us for the first time to perform the data processing necessary to take us to the next level of audit productivity and efficiency. Keep in mind that a state-of-the-art personal computer back then, before competition drove prices down, represented a significant investment. Our tech-oriented initiative also required us to invest in additional equipment like a tape drive so that we could start receiving data directly from clients.

Those old school reel-to-reel tapes were how we received our first data set when we performed the Grand Union grocery audit. We ended up renting a second apartment in the Clocktower, the Connecticut apartment complex where Robert and I were living that also housed our administrative office and very first "data center," which initially consisted of a single IBM PC. In time, we ran out of room and had to rent a third apartment. That one doubled as Larry's crash pad whenever he was in town.

There were plenty of changes taking place within a short amount of time. Being much younger than our principals gave Larry and me an opportunity to experience the power of the new and emerging PC technology firsthand. Having worked at ComputerLand, Larry was well versed in PC computing power, and I had already secured a few victories myself, programming database software like dBASE III to complete the Target manifest audit. Being married to a computer genius helped too. Our investments in PC technology became one of those fortuitous decisions that allowed us not only to compete but ultimately to become a technology leader in our industry.

THE UNDERDOG'S COMPETITIVE ADVANTAGE

We knew that computers could make the manual side of audit work much easier. I saw it during the Target freight project and again with the Walmart account. It was time for us to take advantage of technology with our entire approach to auditing.

One option we tested was asking clients to run reports for us. This approach presented immediate problems because client tech departments were already swamped. The last thing they had capacity for was supporting contractors like us. For those that were willing to create reports for us, we still had no option but to operate within their time frames. We had to wait for the data to be delivered, and then, if the reports were incorrect, we had to wait for modifications to be completed.

It was a pain point we could not allow to affect our relationships or our ability to complete assignments in a timely way. We had to find a way to gather data while being sensitive to the amount of time we required from our clients' resources. That led to a second option, hiring a third party to manage the data for us. But that option meant succumbing to variability and cost inconsistency in the output from the various third parties we would engage.

We had to find a way to gather data while being sensitive to the amount of time we required from our clients' resources.

Behind door number three was the golden opportunity for us: roll up our sleeves and get into the technology game by doing it ourselves. We chose to go for sweat equity. It had served us well in the past, and we expected no less as we ventured into the realm of acquiring, building, and developing our own technology capabilities.

There were a few mountains to climb at first. In the early '90s, it wasn't very common for companies to share their proprietary data with external vendors; data was considered way too sensitive. Eyebrows were raised when a prospective company looked over our client list and saw two or three of their biggest competitors. We had to persuade them we would act responsibly with their data. We were tasked with convincing clients that the benefits vastly outweighed the risks. One key selling point was that the data we received was from accounts settled years prior, which meant there was little, if anything, a competitor could actually do with the dated information. It worked.

Of course, we went to great lengths to make sure we kept client data protected. Eventually, the negotiation process went from persuasion to a standard capability that clients expected. They looked for companies with the resources and advanced expertise to mine their data. Having technology capability quickly became a prerequisite to landing accounts, and the game quickly became how you could distinguish yourself from the competition and demonstrate that *your* technology was *better*.

PRG and Schultz chose to build their foundation on promoting the capabilities of their mainframe technology. After investing tens of millions of dollars in intricate computer systems, they boasted about their ability to crunch a ton of transactions at once. I'm sure they saw it as an advantage over companies like CCA. In fact, they wouldn't even mention us by name when listing their competition. They looked at it like a numbers game. Their approach was along the lines of, "These mom-and-pops haven't made the investments that we have. How could they ever compare?"

To them, CCA was an underdog to be discounted, but privately, we were seeing a lot of success performing secondary audits. Of course, being the secondary on an account is a little harder than executing a primary audit. Secondary reviews required you to do all the work of the primary and still find incremental results. We had to get creative to produce better results to find the incremental improper payments the primary missed. It's harder to do the work, and more expensive, unless you have the tool set to be faster and more efficient as a secondary. Over time, clients would begin to recognize that to perform well on a secondary was a difficult challenge, and that a firm that could perform well on a secondary could also perform well in the primary position. Ultimately this helped pave the way for us to move into the primary position at many of our accounts, resulting in increased market share.

Still, the time came to take our business from good to great. We wanted to be the best in the industry, not in size but in performance. Our success was dependent on our ability to find the right person to see us through. Robert became the perfect man for the job, in more ways than one.

Robert was always interested in computers. His fascination was no different from the way kids today find themselves attached to their video games. While he was in high school, it was just a hobby for him. He learned more about programming, and eventually, there was no doubt in his mind about what he wanted to study in college. Fortunately, he stayed on what seemed to be his destined course.

Robert used some of the money he saved from working odd jobs through high school and college, a mix of construction and computer consulting work, to sponsor a once-in-a-lifetime Hawaiian adventure to celebrate getting his degree. He came back with a renewed sense of confidence. Whatever he did, his mind and his hands were always at work. After college, he worked as a programmer for two firms before starting his own company. His first few years in the industry happened to align with the time when personal computers really started to take the small business world by storm.

Everyone was implementing or expanding their initial computer systems. Everyone had the personal computer on their radar. You couldn't get away from them. His interest turned into a passion, which evolved into a thriving opportunity. Robert's familiarity afforded him the chance to work with small businesses, helping them install computer systems. He handled everything from hardware, software, and network support to hardwiring—anything the business needed.

The rise in PC popularity also meant that computers were becoming cheaper. The problem was, even with such a steady demand, people for the most part did not know how to use them. That's where Robert's expertise came into the equation.

Eventually, Alexander Systems started to earn a few major accounts. Robert's services were contracted by a large law firm in Danbury, Connecticut, and an established real estate development company in Stamford. CCA was the next to be added to his list of exclusive clientele.

Robert had a level of intellect and understanding about things that went beyond our expertise. His keen business sense and proven ability quickly turned him into our understated secret weapon.

He was the third leg of the stool, so to speak, who supported Larry and me in our quest to grow the business. He contracted with us for a year or so before agreeing to sell Alexander Systems, allowing him to come work for CCA full time. This was a pivotal moment for our company because without Robert's involvement, CCA would never have accomplished the growth and market leadership we achieved as a result of his technology vision and execution. With his help, CCA became known as a data-mining expert—at least that was the term used in the early 2000s, when big data became a thing. Eventually, we would be known as a data analytics company, and "audit recovery" would no longer be descriptive enough to explain all we could do. We never would have been able to achieve that had Robert not signed on.

When he joined us in March 1993, that's when the real fun started. Building systems. Loading data. Programming. Running reports. He did everything we needed to automate and scale our business, and in the beginning, he did it all by himself.

We intrinsically trusted him to deliver. There is a book called *The Speed of Trust,* written by Stephen M. R. Covey, that explains the value of trust. If you trust the people you work with, you can accelerate what you are trying to accomplish. Our business benefited immensely from the trust we placed in Robert and his ability to deliver the technology we needed to compete.

PLACING FAITH IN TECHNOLOGY

Through the 1990s and beyond, data and computers were utterly transformative for our industry. With the evolution of our auditing methods and the proprietary tools we developed, we could take data and slice and dice it to look for anomalies, mining the data for errors we never could have previously recognized manually. Led by Robert, we placed tremendous faith in how technology could transform our business. Had we listened to those resistant to change, we would not have made cohesive advancements when technology took over the industry. At some point, the value of paper documents basically vanished into thin air as electronic data interchange (EDI) files became the norm. There were no more warehouses where we could set up those classic brown folding tables and sift through old files.

New data types such as internal emails between buyers and vendors were eventually added to the equation, along with other unstructured electronic data sets, and if you did not have the capability to sift through them, you could not perform. For example, all we needed was a SKU number, and we could search for corresponding deals through various client emails and attachments, giving us access to hard-to-find information.

Every client was different. They had different data systems, and even when using a packaged financial system such as SAP or Oracle Financials, each implementation varied from another. Recognizing no two client data sets were the same, we knew our technology approach had to become flexible. We did not try to force fit a client's data set into a preexisting format. Our flexibility philosophy was the root of our success. CCA was able to stay ahead of the curve because our technology strategy could adapt so easily. It was also affordable and easy to customize and scale.

CCA was able to stay ahead of the curve because our technology strategy could adapt so easily. It was also affordable and easy to customize and scale.

We ran with the power of PCs from day one, and by the time our competitors realized the limiting functionality of mainframe systems, we were already ten years down the road. Quite simply, we figured out how to receive and process large volumes of data from many different types of systems. We created reports and built all sorts of proprietary technology tools to help our field auditors mine the multiple terabytes of data we ultimately received, allowing us to find the most money possible in the shortest amount of time.

BUILDING OUR TECHNOLOGY FUNCTION

Robert gave us the technology pathway to succeed. Unlike the one-off attempt at integrating technology we used at Walmart from 1985 to 1987, his strategy was solid. It was something we could scale and replicate for all our clients. We knew fusing technology into our business model was something that had to be done. We knew we *could* do it, but if it was going to be successful, we had to make a change as a company.

In the past, how an audit was executed was entirely up to the principal. Each principal had the freedom to decide how they wanted to run their audit; they were the captains of their own ships, and their crew was made up entirely of independent contractors. The only thing that kept us together as an organization was our aligned contingency and commission-based business model. But with growth and expansion in mind, we knew we needed a unified approach. Eventually, we announced that, moving forward, anyone working on a CCA audit would have to use CCA technology and our data center to process client data.

At first, there were objections. Our principals were used to having the freedom to hire their own resources and process data however they saw fit. They especially didn't like the idea of having to pay CCA for data services that some felt they could manage better on their own. But not having a centralized technology function for the entire company would seriously limit CCA's ability to scale.

We held to our decision despite many who weren't convinced we had the best approach or the experience to make the technology work. Although the change meant infringing on some of the perks of being independent contractors, we needed people to adapt and had to have faith in what we felt was necessary. We understood there was resistance. Everything we were presenting to them was entirely new, and they didn't necessarily have the confidence we had that Robert could deliver. The strategy we put on the table had no track record to prove it would work. Many of the principals thought, "What makes you think you can tell me how to perform my audit better than I could?" Despite the objections, we stuck to our guns. We announced that Connolly was taking a new direction and needed to create a standard approach, regardless of where the audits were taking place.

The goal was to be more competitive than ever before. We knew that the technology model would allow us to share our knowledge by creating competencies that could transfer from one client to another.

With that said, we did not get it right on the first try. We modified our initial computer policy several times before we got to a place that made everyone comfortable. We had staff threatening to revolt—well, not literally, but they probably wished they could have. We heard their concerns and managed through them.

Now in full effect, these changes required us to add equipment to the makeshift data center Robert had built in the apartments we were renting in the Clocktower. More equipment meant greater investments, which meant we had to charge our people to recoup costs. Robert was working hard to refine our algorithms to make them as efficient as possible, knowing that time had value also.

His first goal was to answer questions like:

- What software should we be using to read the tapes?

- What's the best way to decode it?

- How do you translate this data?

- How do we present the data to the auditors?

The data we received needed to be processed and arranged in a certain format. Our process and tool sets were built, rebuilt, tweaked, and adjusted, but the result was always on the crest of what we needed.

The Grand Union audit was the test run that helped us put things into perspective. Based out of New Jersey, Grand Union was the first client data set we ever processed. We didn't even have our own tape drive yet and had to outsource the work to a third-party data-processing center. It was new to us at first, but later, once we overcame the challenge of reading data off tapes, we were able to perfect the PC auditing niche.

As the strategy worked, we eventually hired more people to help Robert build out his vision. Robert knew computers inside and out, but two of his first hires magnified his impact. Michael Matloub, credited with building much of our internal accounting systems and the queries or algorithms used to look for overpayments, and Tony Massanelli, hired on from PRG for his knowledge about auditing specifics and tool set development, tripled the effectiveness of Robert's contribution. Together, the three of them worked to create more front-end tools and helped us shift to online auditing.

Because of what they created, we were able to move away from the hassle of printing reports and delivering them to auditors. As the PC became more powerful, so did our technological abilities and our desire to put the power of technology in the hands of our auditors. Ironically enough, when Tony reached out to Robert for an interview, his father was still the CIO for PRG. We took that as a sign that anything was possible, especially if you had a strong strategy and solid team.

> *As the PC became more powerful, so did our technological abilities and our desire to put the power of technology in the hands of our auditors.*

INFINITE POSSIBILITIES

We once had a client task us with an impossible deadline. They agreed to hire us as the secondary on the account but gave us only a few months to produce our findings. Like many clients in those earlier years, they were concerned about the idea of vendors looking at their data but curious about what might be found. Even with the clock running, the flexibility of our technology approach allowed us to perform in the short time window, and the audit was a success.

As we grew, data was flooding in from different sources, and we needed to scale. One computer turned into two. One type of tape drive eventually became another. We tweaked and refined our data center so that it could process clients' data in virtually any format. Sometimes we needed reels. Other audits called for cassettes. We bought servers—lots and lots of servers—and they became faster and faster.

Eventually, the time came for us to move our equipment out of that hot apartment building into a more formal setting. We rented our first commercial office space at High Ridge Park in Stamford, Connecticut, in 1993 to serve as Connolly's data center and administrative office. Our first server room was more like a meat locker there, an oversized closet to house our computers, kept cold by a barrier of plastic sheeting in place of a door, just like you'd see at a butcher's shop. Once again, Robert got to work. He and his team did everything from arranging computers to assembling homemade server racks.

Soon thereafter growth required that we move to a new location in the same building, with a purpose-built computer room with a raised floor. Later, when the offices moved to Wilton, Connecticut, we built an even bigger computer room with more racks than we ever thought we would need, along with appropriate cooling and backup power. But we quickly outgrew that space as well and eventually added even more capacity with another off-site data center in Darien, Connecticut. With the steady stream of new data coming our way, we soon had to build a data center in a separate facility in Norwalk, Connecticut, which is still in use today. Of interest is that we were running a private "cloud" computing environment long before cloud computing became commonplace.

Despite all the growth, expansion, and opportunity, we continued to maintain a very measured approach. We only made incremental changes and verified each adjustment before adding on. This wasn't something that was budgeted or planned out to the letter. If Robert said we needed new equipment, we trusted his word and put the order in.

Early on, IT was not a mission-critical part of the business. If a company's IT team stopped functioning for a few weeks, things would not have been noticeably disrupted. Eventually, clients wanted to know that we could help them stay afloat in the event that a server crashed or there was some other type of disturbance. That's why the redundant data centers were so important. Half of the business ran through one location and the other half in another. If something happened to one data center, we only needed to load a single location. Robert helped us develop a footprint that not only kept our operation sustainable but allowed us to process hundreds of millions of rows of data daily for some of the largest healthcare payers and retailers in the world.

AUTOMATING YOUR MISSION

As Robert would say, "How do you build a house? One nail at a time." We started performing more computer work, processing more data, and integrating more advanced analytics. Growth presented its own set of issues. We evolved from a single computer to a larger PC and eventually racks and racks of servers to help us perform our audits.

No one could predict when the next major shift would strike the industry. Initially, Robert had taken on the assignment with CCA with the next four to five years in mind. Nobody could even begin to imagine what the next few decades would eventually bring us. Until then, we focused on giving the opportunity in front of us our undivided attention.

It was a big watershed moment in 1999 when we won the Target account back, followed soon by a promotion to primary in 2002. After shifting our equipment out of the air-conditioned closet to the fully equipped computer room Robert created for us, we presented a more professional face to the world. Target was a major account at the time, and before they signed on, they wanted to visit our data center to see our technology capability at work. Stepping into the facility and seeing our systems for themselves was more than enough proof that CCA was anything but a mom-and-pop business. Next, it was time to automate our execution in the field.

"Give the auditors what they want."

That became the mantra Robert established for the CCA data center. He understood the auditors were the ones driving our accounts, they were the ones who knew where to look for issues, and they knew the issues we needed technology to solve. If we gave the auditors what they needed, they could multiply our results.

Automating the "Connolly way" was easier than for most companies because our flexible system was built around an entire data set, not just bits and pieces. As a result, we did not need to reload data whenever the auditors came to us with a new request. This approach helped us build momentum, and then we automated more areas. For example, once a data query was established for one audit, it was relatively simple to apply it on another audit.

Then came the realization we could be even more efficient if we placed data analysts in the field alongside the audit teams working on our major accounts. This way the audit team could have access to their own personal programmer on site. That level of direct communication eliminated the delay caused by back-and-forth calls to the data center. Auditors no longer needed to wait to receive whatever they requested to be sent to them; the data analyst could address the issue right then and there.

When time is money, a small adjustment such as this could increase our speed and performance while eliminating the bottleneck caused by a flood of requests. Even if there wasn't an analyst on site, we never made our field team submit tickets; everything was always handled on demand. If that meant we received dozens of phone calls a day, then so be it. "Give the auditors what they need."

That momentous Target promotion was our first opportunity to test the data analyst theory. We wanted to see the impact on recoveries when an auditor had an analyst sitting over their shoulder, watching them try to perform a specific task. It was incredible to witness the shift in performance when the analyst could quickly deliver what the auditor needed on the spot. Target became a large marquee primary account for us, one that proved what we could do. We set out to produce remarkable recoveries and hoped our performance at Target would lead to other major promotions.

It worked. We soon earned a promotion at Best Buy. Walmart followed shortly after, as did a string of others. Our reputation as the "nice little secondary firm" soon changed, and we quickly became the top US retail primary recovery audit firm.

People, process, and technology. That was what we were all about.

People, process, and technology. That was what we were all about.

THE COMPETITION TAKES NOTICE

By 1996, PRG went public and took off right along with the dot-com boom that took the nation by storm. This historic economic bubble led to extreme growth nationwide, as society ramped up its use and adaptation of all forms of technology like the internet, personal computing, notebooks, car phones, cell phones, and more. Noticing the opportunity, companies were busy trying to expand their market share. Money was flowing, but those companies were still struggling with integrating new technologies. Eventually, John Cook became one of many CEOs trapped by a roll-up strategy that ultimately didn't work financially.

At one point Cook realized perhaps his best bet was to take CCA out of the arena just as he'd eliminated so many others by buying them out. In fact, in just two short years, PRG and Cook had bought a total of eleven competitors. Our meeting with PRG in 1999 to discuss the possible sale of CCA to them was hard to forget. Larry, Rob, and I met John Cook, Vice Chair Jack Toma, and CFO Michael Lustig in a conference room at the Atlanta airport to discuss their interest in buying CCA. They had just bought another company, Beck and Associates, so we thought the offer might be worth exploring. There we were, tucked off in the airport, waiting for PRG to start their pitch. The exact details of the conversation are fuzzy now, but we all recall how abruptly the meeting came to a hard stop after Robert, in true Robert fashion, skipped the formalities and cut straight to the chase.

He interjected with something like, "Would you be willing to pay fifty million dollars for our business?"

There it was. He laid a number on the line that made everyone's chins drop to the floor. Now that there was no longer any room for the usual meeting preamble, PRG had to take a minute to process their shock and adjust to how forthcoming Robert was.

After regrouping, they coolly told us that $50 million was absolutely out of the question. It is hilarious now—maybe not so much at the time—but I suppose it was exactly what we needed. There was no point in wasting any more time. Either they were willing to pay an exorbitant amount of money to get us out of the game, or we were going to continue on our mission. Since the dollar amount we asked for was out of the question for them and their shareholders, we then said our thank-yous and parted ways.

I'll admit, it was not the most gracious way to handle the exchange, and it led to a bit of a sour taste in the air. All bad feelings aside, we owned the decision to shoot down the pitch because we truly believed in what we could accomplish as a business on our own.

PRG approached *us* with the idea of buying us out; it was completely unsolicited. They saw us as just another mom-and-pop, but we felt CCA was different. We had the technological capability, a great business model, a great client list, and a strong track record of delivering results. We believed in what we had created, and Larry, Rob, and I were young. The business had yet to be valued, and the 1–2x revenue multiple PRG was offering was not all that exciting.

We knew better. We knew CCA could achieve more, if we just continued the strategies that had carried us that far. Robert's $50 million offer was the premium we would've taken to walk away, but PRG did not see our future the way we did that justified the premium we were requesting. To them, less competition meant greater potential for success.

Declining the offer meant the "grow or die" strategy was in full effect. Even without acquiring CCA, PRG was still advancing like an incredible force, as was Howard Schultz, which meant we needed to work even harder to maintain our position.

Declining the offer meant the "grow or die" strategy Larry had first presented at the close of our end-of-the-year review held in January 1997 was in full effect.

Ultimately, PRG paid the price for failing to fully understand the implications of their acquisitions. The company's valuation dropped from the $450 million they held in their heyday to barely registering at $100 million. The stock price drop occurred after PRG acquired Schultz in 2002 and the acquisition struggled to reach the synergy the two companies anticipated. The move allowed PRG to eliminate a major competitor, but it cost the company valuable market share. Of course, they've since recouped some of those losses. CCA chose not to bow down like some of our competitors, but no one could have predicted such a drastic market shift in the coming years. In time, we picked up the secondary audit on many of their accounts where an overlap existed between Schultz and PRG, giving us the opportunity to advance to primary at many of those same accounts as well. CCA was fortunate enough to be well positioned to pick up the pieces when PRG-Schultz stumbled. We were focused on completing quality audits and outperforming the competition, a focus that was recognized—and appreciated—by our clients.

Our trek into the technological era ultimately became the audit recovery translation of David and Goliath. By 2005, we were the ones talking to PRG about selling to *us*. I'm sure it was not the most celebrated moment in John Cook's career, but it was a defining milestone for our business.

We watched as PRG's stock dipped from its high of $160 per share to below $10.00 by the time we had that conversation.[17] At the time, PRG's technology strategy could not scale and deliver support in the way that we could. We eventually opted against making an offer to PRG, after deciding they were too expensive and there was too much of an overlap in our clientele.

For the purposes of this memoir, I asked Robert how it feels to know that he singlehandedly pioneered the technological strategy that CCA maintained for decades to come. It was eye opening for him to recognize how something that began as a hobby in his teens eventually became the foundation of our business's success. As modest as he is, he confessed that he never thought about it that way. Instead, he was quick to point out that what was created couldn't have been done without Mike MatLoub or Tony Massanelli and the many others who were part of our talented IT and data services teams.. "I was incredibly lucky to be working with them. Their expertise in software development and audit technology was critical to Connolly's IT success." In hindsight, he felt good "to know that you can get paid to do something you love, something that benefited your family and countless others."

---

17   Yahoo Finance.

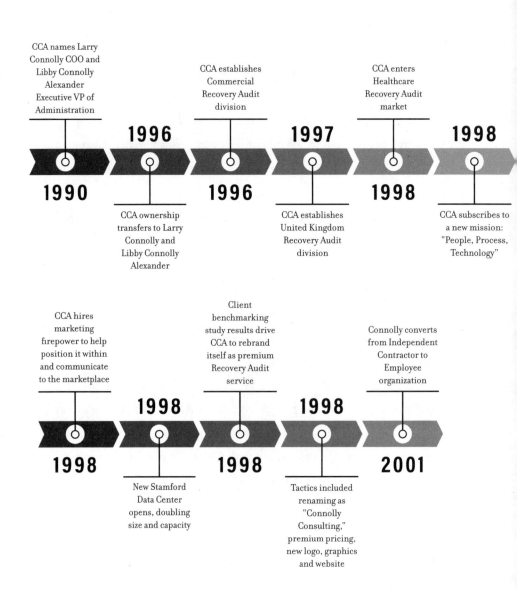

CCA names Larry Connolly COO and Libby Connolly Alexander Executive VP of Administration

CCA establishes Commercial Recovery Audit division

CCA enters Healthcare Recovery Audit market

1996

1997

1998

1990

1996

1998

CCA ownership transfers to Larry Connolly and Libby Connolly Alexander

CCA establishes United Kingdom Recovery Audit division

CCA subscribes to a new mission: "People, Process, Technology"

CCA hires marketing firepower to help position it within and communicate to the marketplace

Client benchmarking study results drive CCA to rebrand itself as premium Recovery Audit service

Connolly converts from Independent Contractor to Employee organization

1998

1998

1998

1998

2001

New Stamford Data Center opens, doubling size and capacity

Tactics included renaming as "Connolly Consulting," premium pricing, new logo, graphics and website

CHAPTER 6

Charting Our Own Course

Making Executive Decisions

Anyone can have good instincts, you just have to be willing
to listen to your inner voice when it's talking to you.

—Libby Connolly Alexander

A t the time we took over, Larry was only thirty-six years old, and I was just thirty. Our father entrusted us with his life's work, the legacy he created through sheer will and determination. Drawing from lessons we'd learned from him in our youth, we were committed to living up to his expectations. It was far from clear that the future would be bright; CCA was small and competing against much more experienced leaders of more sophisticated, well-established organizations.

It takes courage to take on new roles and responsibilities at such a young age, especially when those responsibilities require you to make executive decisions for a business that was considered an underdog in its industry. Yet even without the funding, resources, scale, and market share our competitors had, Connolly had something better. We learned the business from one of the greatest teachers we ever could've asked for. We were determined to keep pushing the business forward. Faith in our business model and our tech strategy kept us focused and motivated.

In the same respect, our future was still uncertain. Connolly needed to find new avenues of growth and new markets, which led us to expand into the UK , Commercial (non-retail) and later Canadian markets. Some of our pursuits were less successful: we attempted to penetrate Germany, and we experimented with a number of strategic alliances in the areas of telecom and tax auditing. Though we saw some success internationally, our future was uncertain. From our small size and the strength of our established competitors, we knew that we had to prepare the business to stand against much more sophisticated organizations.

Our advancement into technology solidified our belief in what we could accomplish by taking calculated risks. We learned from experience and knew that, even in our new leadership role, we would need to continue evolving. Each situation was evaluated independently, and we did our best to construct the most appropriate response. Most times, we came out ahead, but there were quite a few instances where we placed wrong bets. Through it all, we had to learn to follow our internal compass and do the best we could with the resources we had available.

We were resourceful. We weren't going to cop out on our responsibilities under the guise of age or leadership inexperience. Our clients depended on us to deliver, and the folks that worked for us depended on us for job security. We handled our responsibilities with the same focus Jim Connolly instilled in us all our lives. "If you work on it long enough, eventually, you'll figure it out."

Our technology was in place and steadily advancing. We had a strong list of blue-chip clients, and we were winning business and having some success expanding internationally, especially in the UK. The top line was growing. The next thing we needed to consider was how to differentiate and represent CCA as a brand. We were facing fierce competition in the marketplace against established global players, and clients were starting to view the industry as a commodity. We had to take another risk and try something different. Fortunately, there were a few options that were worth considering.

We saw the need to invest in talent as much as we'd invested in clients and technology. We realized we needed marketing expertise to solidify our brand and market position through a strategy that would keep us memorable and relevant. And we needed experienced sales professionals to take our message to the market. This realization came at a time in the company's history when we needed to hire more than bodies; we needed to hire skills. We were looking for people with the expertise that we didn't have. This went for every department throughout the company. We knew we needed specific skills to thrive.

Through it all, we had to learn to follow our internal compass and do the best we could with the resources we had available.

MAKING THE RIGHT INVESTMENTS

Traditional business guides would say that we did things all wrong. They'll tell you to begin by spending time scribing out a formal mission statement, vision, and core values. We did not do any of that. At least, not at first. We were entrepreneurs. We really subscribed to the practice of making decisions from the head, the heart, and the gut.

We had a big competitor—PRG—that just went public, and at the same time, we found ourselves competing against smaller companies like Loder Drew, who had stormed the nonretail market when everybody else was sleeping. The nature of securing new business was also changing. No longer were our veteran principals able to rely on relationships and connections to win new clients. Corporations that hired us at the time were beginning to think all competitors in our industry were the same, a commodity where price is the only differentiator. Connolly not only needed to sell but also needed to position ourselves in the market for the first time so we could go head to head with the competition. After that, we needed to initiate a plan that would solidify our market position.

We knew we had a powerful product, but we had to ask ourselves if that was being represented in our branding and market presence. That made Kevin Clark, our first official marketing employee, the next investment in human capital that vastly benefited the business.

Before Kevin was hired, we found ourselves back in that place where we knew something needed to be done but did not fully understand *what* or *why*. In the beginning, we nagged him to explain exactly *what* a marketing executive did. It's a running joke between us now, but back then, it was important for us to take measured steps. Like many entrepreneurs, we confused sales with marketing. Kevin helped us understand that long term, your position in the market—how your current and potential customers perceive you—is paramount if you wish to retain the customers you have and add new ones. Eventually, he did more than prove *why* we needed him around.

Moving through the '90s, procurement became a new intermediary, and requests for proposals (RFPs) became a new standard. It started with nonretail, but eventually all lines of business were looking to purchase our service as if we were pencils and pens, a commodity. At the same time, the competition was as intense as ever, and people like Kevin were the investments that would allow us to continue to meet the markets' new demands.

Differentiating ourselves and carefully planning our positioning was paramount for us. Connolly spent a lot of time upholding our reputation in private, but now it was time to tell our story to the broader market. We needed to get the word out there. The relationships our clients had with CCA were moving beyond handshake agreements, and procurement departments, with their RFPs and bidding contests, required us to dedicate significant time and resources to participate in new account solicitations with no promise the effort would be rewarded with new business. RFPs held sway over what had previously been a simple and short sales process.

At the same time, we saw the success Loder Drew and another competitor, Apex Analytix, were having penetrating markets outside of retail, and we wanted to build a nonretail beachhead where we perceived incremental growth potential.

We were already seeing success with nonretail companies like Eastman Kodak, and we had just finished a massive RFP and successful procurement process for AT&T. Although we made little money from our AT&T contract, we saw surprising success with AT&T Wireless, a division of AT&T. The nonretail environment was filled with lots of promise, and Connolly wanted to tap into that opportunity. We just had to put the resources in place to capitalize on the opportunity even though we were late to the game.

PEOPLE, PROCESS, AND TECHNOLOGY

As you can see, CCA had quite a few things going for us at the same time. By 1998, our focus on developing the company's new strategy evolved into the need to segment a new mission that concentrated on three things: *people*, *process*, and *technology*. If our company was to be successful, we needed all three gears working at capacity. We were already investing in our infrastructure by hiring the right people. Larry and I were handling the operational side of things, the process. Robert and his team had just opened our brand-new data center, doubling in size and capacity and securing our technology capability. Then Kevin came in to help us tell our story through branding and positioning.

> *People, process, and technology. If our company was to be successful, we needed all three gears working at capacity.*

The numbers were already telling a story in themselves. Kevin initiated a client survey that showed the company's satisfaction and retention rates were off the charts. We were receiving stellar reviews across the board, and our client relationships were sound, proving that our business was as strong as ever. Kevin helped us to recognize we were first and foremost a *people* business. He also used the results of the client satisfaction survey to demonstrate that we were a *premium brand*, not a commodity, and deserved to charge more than the competition. He led us to change our name from the nondescript acronym CCA to Connolly Consulting, and later just Connolly. The change demonstrated we were about people and that our quality results warranted putting our family name on the business.

connolly consulting associates
recovery audit specialists

At the same time that we changed our name, we also hired outside resources to help us totally redo our logo, corporate identity, and website. Our new logo design incorporated what we referred to as an eyebrow, two swooshes that intersected over the Connolly name. The swooshes reflected our belief that superior results were delivered through the intersection of our two greatest strengths: exceptional people and outstanding technology.

Our results by this time were truly impressive. We had a 97 percent client satisfaction rate and a 98 percent client retention rate. The only clients we ever lost were the ones we fired! The client satisfaction surveys Kevin produced also proved our "quality results / low noise" approach was one of the reasons our clients loved us.

We viewed Connolly as an extension of our clients. We weren't about breaking glass and putting our priorities in front of our clients. We endeavored to go about our work without disruption, meaning we conducted our audits with the clients' needs in mind. Vendor relationships, whether large or small, are sensitive. We were thorough but adopted the mantra "There is no money in a bad claim," which helped us build credibility while avoiding unproductive disputes. This turned out to be a key selling point that resonated well with our clients.

Working on contingency was sensitive, and it was important to remain cognizant of that. On the one hand, the billions of dollars of recoveries we generated on behalf of our clients were material and impacted their bottom lines. On the other, we were dealing with their valued suppliers, basically contacting them to say, "Hey, you owe our client money, and oh by the way, this is from a few years back." This was typically money the vendor wasn't reserving when they had settled their books long ago. Money they did not budget to repay. Yet CCA knew how to handle these discussions. No shortcuts. We always felt a properly explained and well-documented claim would make it easier for a supplier to accept, even if they didn't like the outcome.

This approach earned us trust and long-term relationships. Moving forward, we assembled a marketing and sales plan that aligned with our yearly objectives. Concentrating on nonretail prospects, we identified what would become the threshold of the "tall-building strategy." Using this as our guide, we stopped going after companies ("short buildings") with annuals sales of less than $5 billion. There were bigger fish in the sea, so we cast our nets in their direction. To help us progress, we hired a director of sales, Tom Santacroce, in 2002, to pioneer our nonretail development. Earlier we had moved principal talent—Howard Flaum and Lloyd Parsons—over to help in this area. They now reported to Tom.

EMERGENCE OF THE IAPP

Our involvement with the International Accounts Payable Professionals (IAPP) organization was our next major marketing move. The IAPP gave us direct access to prospective clients in all the market verticals we were pursuing, which made it a prime opportunity to solicit new clients. We were involved with local chapters and also attended the organization's annual conference. This trade show was an excellent way for us to support and entertain existing clients. At its peak, the conference was fairly large, with several thousand attendees each year, in contrast to its modest beginning. We recognized its potential and learned to adapt to the opportunity, which meant investing for the first time in trade show booths, sponsorship, and entertainment.

Connolly always had a client-prospect event at the trade show, and we worked hard to make it very memorable. You can imagine how these events encouraged a game of one-upmanship between competitors. We were all like proud peacocks fluttering our feathers, trying to differentiate ourselves. It just so happened that Connolly's feathers were a bit more attractive, or at least I always thought so.

We battled to plan the better venue for our client party and create an environment where our guests could have the most fun. The IAPP conference became an event that people anticipated all year, and they continued talking about it until the next one. Our main attraction was a fabulous magician named David Harris, who would draw in the crowd to our booth with his captivating personality. Kevin had met David at an Orlando restaurant and recognized his potential to attract IAPP show attendees to our booth. We maintained our relationship with David for many, many years, and many viewed David as an extension of us. That relationship went a step further as an example and metaphor for the way Connolly valued the people we worked with. He eventually became the crowd's main attraction. David was much more fun than a magician; he was also a marketing messenger that could perform some outstanding tricks.

Each year, we covered all the bases. Connolly always had a premiere position in the exhibit hall. We also sponsored some amazing speakers, which gave us an opportunity to introduce them in front of the entire crowd. For years, I'd get up on stage and offer a shameless (but subtle) sales pitch before welcoming keynote speakers like Jerry Lewis and Connie Podesta to the audience.

When it was first launched in the early '90s by former AT&T accounts payable manager, Nelda Barkley, the IAPP was the only industry event of its kind. It started as just a group of people in a hotel ballroom, but it multiplied over time. There was no better way to promote the Connolly brand than in a conference filled with the largest corporations in America. It was more than the opportunity to shoot our shot; it gave us a bit of social time with our clients at a time when corporate governance made that harder and harder. Formal business meetings always presented a level of defensiveness with clients. Out of the office, clients were more relaxed, and connecting on a personal level was easier. They were often reluctant to be entertained, but the IAPP helped us express our gratitude for their business and give them an experience they would always remember.

ESTABLISHING A NEW SALES CAPABILITY

Our focus on growth and expansion meant we needed to reconsider the way we approached the sales process. Previously, nearly all of our sign-ons with new clients were done with a handshake. You would talk with a representative from the company, a contract would be drawn, and then we went off to execute the agreement. Things changed when procurement began managing the contracting process and the market adopted the request for proposal (RFP) procedure. First and foremost, the goal was to get invited to bid. Once on the bidders list, we would need to differentiate ourselves and show best value.

When the recovery audit industry went digital, there were no more faith-based deals and agreements based on mutual understandings. For a time, the market slid into an internet bidding contest. The idea of throwing vendors into the gauntlet and forcing them to lower their rates in a reverse auction even tempted some existing clients. At the end of the contract, they no longer simply signed a renewal. Procurement would get involved, wanting to see what opening an RFP could achieve. All we put into creating extensive written requests was redirected to online bidding platforms like Ariba, and we had to battle it out regardless of our tenured relationships and proven track records. This process had the effect of neutralizing all relationship dividends.

Despite the hours of preparation, I'm almost convinced that most of the time procurement never even read our RFP responses, documents we invested tremendous time and effort to complete. Instead, I suspect their eyes went straight to the rates. Clients understood the value of finding a recovery audit partner that could present the whole package, but procurement never had an issue with staging specific rules for a contract. Many went as far as to spell it out for us: "This bid will be awarded based on price only." Treating us like a commodity worked to their advantage, at least when it came to price.

It was a challenging time for service providers. We were handling roughly fifty RFPs per year, yet we still managed to hold our rates high relative to the competition. We worked hard to illustrate our premium brand position with prospects and to demonstrate that, while Connolly asked for a higher fee, we produced better results. We would back our claims up with testimonials and client examples. Even so, selling value was not easy for us.

After our first RFP with AT&T in 1996, we understood more about how the procurement-run contracting process worked. It was a turning point for our sales approach. We realized we needed a plan to adjust. It was evident that we would not be having any more two-martini lunches with clients and prospects! Companies decided that being wined and dined was influencing their decisions, so they inserted a rigid, unvested procurement team to act in their interest.

This forced us to schedule hours of work, sometimes days even, to put these RFPs together. We drudged through them on our own at first, but then we had no choice but to invest in someone like the talented and creative Susan Meller, a key marketing hire, who could handle them for us. Developing a strong competency in RFP writing was another critical investment in our future. Once again, people, process, and technology held Connolly together.

RECOGNIZING YOUR OWN VALUE

From day one, Connolly benefited from a bottom-up model. If our auditors were successful, then our principals were successful. If the principals were successful, our clients were successful. And the clients' success translated into our own.

We had to pay attention to situations that would not be a winning scenario for our auditors. The online reverse auction bidding we were seeing created times when the rates got so low that we knew we couldn't be successful. That's when we had to consider the benefits of saying no. It is one thing to try to get a client just for the sake of saying you've signed on a new company and added a logo to your client list, but that was not the way we worked. Whenever we placed a bid, we did so calculating it was going to be a win-win for the client and for Connolly. Our associates were depending on us to assign them to engagements where they could be financially successful. Win-lose scenarios would not do their households any favors.

So there came times when we had to evaluate the pros and cons of a contract, and many times, that meant walking away. Instead of bidding unrealistic rates, we would insert zeros into those spaces for an offer. We just refused to bid. We stood firmly in the fact that Connolly was not a commodity. We were not going to sign on a new client and put our reputation at risk because of the gimmicky game the reverse auction process created.

There was a major new client in Texas that opened a bid, and we had to say, "No, this isn't going to work for our company" and didn't participate. We were put in a similar situation with an existing client and major national grocery chain that opened a bid, and once again, we had to decline the opportunity to participate in their online auction. It took courage, but we weren't going to drive our rates into the ground and back our auditors against the wall with a win-lose agreement where they could not make any money for the work they performed.

Fortunately, companies like ours stood firm, and eventually, that reverse auction trend that emerged in the '90s with Ariba came to a head. Companies started to realize the backlash and began to back away from structuring procurements that could potentially scare away quality bidders. In the meantime, when the competition got fierce, it took courage for Connolly to stand up and have conviction about the value of our service.

Businesses were continuously trying to minimize our value to the point that it was becoming absurd. In that moment, we had to just push back and stand up for our people and our company.

Everybody has been in a place where they had to stop and think, "I knew I should not have done that." Most times, there was some sort of warning or red flag that tried to help us avoid those regrettable circumstances. Even with alarms ringing in our heads, we can be stubborn, especially when means walking away from new business. There's no crystal ball to predict the future, but your inside voice can help you figure out a decision blueprint that works for you. Like the cartoon character Fred Flintstone, everyone has their own little Great Gazoo. If you're smart enough to listen to it, you will know exactly what you should (and should not) decide to do.

Our new marketing plan was a calculated risk. We understood enough to know it was necessary. We knew we had to be smarter than the rest if we were going to survive the competition. The reverse auctions were forcing price wars. We knew there were some procurements where the rates could not be rationalized, and we would have to walk away, as too much risk for our auditors meant too much risk for Connolly. We were already well versed in what it took to have a successful audit engagement. Larry and I spent seven years performing audits in the field. We knew the business. We knew what it took to execute an audit and build good client relationships. Connolly was focused on creating mutually beneficial engagements, on taking assignments that aligned with our personal and professional goals. We measured our success by the way we benefited all those who placed their trust in us. From our clients to our employees, we had to draw a line in the sand to outline our expectations. Doing so set a new standard. It raised the precedent for anyone who considered doing business with us in the future.

FROM IC TO EMPLOYEE

The mother of all calculated risks was accepting the reality that one part of our father's original business model was not going to stand up to Connolly's new direction. After careful consideration, we could not ignore how our new path removed our people from the realm of independent

The mother of all calculated risks was accepting the reality that one part of our father's original business model was not going to stand up to Connolly's new direction.

contractors, at least according to the IRS. Under their rules, there are twenty criteria points one must meet in order to operate under an independent contractor model. Mandating the use of Connolly's data center and tool sets had us tap dancing on the fine line drawn by semantics.

Independent contractors are supposed to be able to supply their own tools of the trade themselves, but the minute we responded to the industry's call for technology, we knew we could not afford to allow our people to continue to do that. It took a lot of planning and consideration, but we finally decided the time had come for us to shift to an employee-based business.

Moving in this direction was the single most important decision we made that allowed the company to standardize, scale, and compete in a way we never could have under the independent contractor model. We knew there was some risk of losing a few good ICs who were married to their independence, but we were prepared to do what was best for Connolly long term. First, we contracted with an outsourced service provider to help us run payroll and human resources. Initially, it seemed like a good idea because it meant less demand on our resources, and quite honestly, we knew nothing about managing an HR department.

The decision to move away from the IC model was finalized and announced in 2000, but we did not implement it until 2001 to avoid causing financial burden from necessary double tax withholding. Some ICs looked at it like the beginning of the end. They feared it meant we would become some sort of autocracy, becoming an also-ran with our competitors. Fortunately, we opted to be as transparent as possible, and January 1, 2001, was relatively uneventful.

Our people understood the environment was changing and why this was the best decision for the company. PRG had already made the switch, so in some ways we weren't setting a new precedent.

Everything we did to scale the business depended on us losing the IC structure. It also aligned with our marketing plans and helped us be consistent with our company culture. Growing in numbers and in territory, we were hiring a lot of new people. Consistency and unifying the company was becoming paramount. We didn't just want to succeed; we wanted to succeed in a manner that was consistent with the new vision we were creating. It was a new day for us. Hiring, firing, offering rewards—everything would soon be anchored around the same values and principles.

There were people joining our ranks who had no previous experience or understanding about the way the business or industry had historically operated. A new hire fresh out of college would look at us with big, bubbly eyes and say, "What do you mean there's a compensation model that doesn't involve a fixed salary?"

If you were not experienced in our industry, the commission

concept seemed too risky, but there were plenty of industry veterans and thankfully new risk takers who appreciated the flexibility and upside potential. We onboarded so many new faces in the early 2000s, and we never would have been able to manage that type of scaling under the original independent contractor model. Having employees was different, but we relied on our culture to prove Connolly was a business that still promoted creativity, curiosity, client focus, and the (partially restrained) entrepreneurial spirit.

We still knew where our success came from, so taking care of our people remained our primary goal. From day one, the business was built from the bottom up.

If our auditors did well, it meant we were producing results for our clients, which made them happy, and that was good news for the company as a whole.

It took a bit of doing and undoing, but we had the business on the right track. New hires meant new ideas, and new ideas usually led to new sources of revenue. In fact, that's exactly what led us into healthcare. It's time to share that maverick of a story. Chapter 7 is where things really start to get interesting.

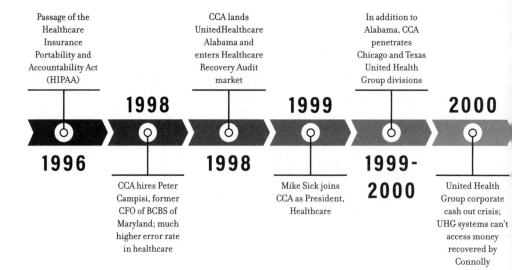

Passage of the Healthcare Insurance Portability and Accountability Act (HIPAA)

CCA lands UnitedHealthcare Alabama and enters Healthcare Recovery Audit market

In addition to Alabama, CCA penetrates Chicago and Texas United Health Group divisions

1998

1999

2000

1996

1998

1999-2000

CCA hires Peter Campisi, former CFO of BCBS of Maryland; much higher error rate in healthcare

Mike Sick joins CCA as President, Healthcare

United Health Group corporate cash out crisis; UHG systems can't access money recovered by Connolly

CHAPTER 7

Scaling to Opportunity

The Healthcare Business

*The best new ideas for making money at Connolly
came from the people who worked for us.*

—Libby Connolly Alexander

T he year was 1998. Larry was down in Atlanta, while I was handling most of the business's back-office functions in Stamford. Connolly was hitting full stride, and the team was putting our heads together to figure out the best plan of attack to activate mission "grow or die." Although things were advancing nicely, there were still a few kinks to work out.

Transitioning from an independent contractor model to an employee-based organization was a major change in our compensation approach. It required us to sort through a number of commission-to-payroll, expense-sharing, reimbursement, and human resources issues we had not dealt with in the past. As a business, Connolly was firing on all cylinders, doing our best to keep up with our own momentum.

That momentum came with a new load of corporate responsibilities. Someone had to step up to manage all of them. That someone became me.

Whether finance or HR, marketing or sales, the hub of our operation fell under my responsibility at our office in Connecticut. And even though Robert was mostly self-managed, IT technically fell under me as well. Connolly was growing consistently, and everyone was still very focused on identifying new opportunities for expansion. Larry and I were both working to grow our core retail business as well as expand into the commercial and international markets like the UK. Our retail clients were well seasoned and performing as nicely as they always had, and we had also recently landed a few nonretail accounts like AT&T, United Technologies, Rohm and Haas, and British Telecom, which presented new types of data for us to deal with.

Our schedules were loaded with things to do, and although it felt like we were being stretched to the max, we could not ignore the unique opportunity that seemingly developed out of thin air.

If you judge what the business ultimately became, you probably would not believe that our initial foray into healthcare was somewhat of an accident. The "grow or die" initiative sent us off to explore nearly every industry, searching for new opportunities. None of us recognized the potential healthcare could offer until we were given the heads-up by one of our newly recruited associates.

Peter Campisi was a former CFO of Blue Cross Blue Shield of Maryland, and we had recently hired him to work in our retail group. In a think-tank-style meeting, his background in healthcare led him to make a trans-formative suggestion. Though he was working under Bob Lancaster on a grocery account in Virginia at the time, Peter recalled the drastic medical claims payment error rate he'd witnessed while working in the healthcare industry.

> *If you judge what the business ultimately became, you probably would not believe that our initial foray into health-care was somewhat of an accident.*

Comparing opportunities, Peter interjected with something along the lines of, "If you think the error rate is significant in the grocery sector, you should see the mess with healthcare claims payments." That was our eureka moment!

Although we were chomping at the bit to realize this potential new opportunity, we were also savvy enough to know healthcare was different. We knew working with personal health information was sensitive, and we had to consider the rapidly changing healthcare market we were entering.

Moving into healthcare meant Connolly would have to make some major adjustments while learning to navigate the mountains of red tape wrapped around the new Health Insurance Portability and Accountability Act (HIPAA), medical claim payment policy, health regulations, new data sets, and so on. With nothing more than a basic understanding of the industry, we had to accept the idea that healthcare would present us with a heaping set of new challenges.

The HIPAA privacy rule had just passed in 1996, and the healthcare industry was still adjusting and very fragmented. Unlike the case of my father, who had embarked on a business concept he saw as already proven, none of us had ever considered reviewing medical claims for improper payments. Even with a "tread carefully" sign plastered above the idea, we could not turn our backs to the fact that, although we knew absolutely nothing about healthcare, there might just be some opportunity there.

It's kind of funny to think Peter's mention of opportunities in healthcare came the same way that he was actually referred to us. Peter was a friend of Ken Stock, an amazing man who joined Connolly when my father was still active. Ken recommended Peter to Larry because he knew his background as a CFO could benefit our business's growth, and Peter was in need of an opportunity. His experience was not in retail, but Connolly was never opposed to pulling talent from unconventional places. We were looking for experience and thought his background in finance was a fit, so Larry hired Peter. Little did we know Peter would be the one to make a casual suggestion that ultimately pivoted the direction of the entire company. Had we turned our backs on Ken's referral, we could have missed out on the chance to work with someone who brought a lot of value to Connolly.

Nothing could have prepared us for what our healthcare division eventually became. Pitching UnitedHealth Group (UHG), the parent corporation for UnitedHealthcare (UHC), its healthcare coverage and benefits platform, and Optum, its information-technology-enabled health services, was another of those examples of Connolly's affinity for taking calculated risks. After exploring the opportunity and considering our options, we decided to pursue the meeting with UHG because, well, why not?

After listening to our team, we realized that healthcare had potential. Peter offered to introduce Connolly to one of his former colleagues who was a divisional CFO for UHC in Birmingham, Alabama. Peter was pretty confident he could arrange a meeting for us. He worked his magic, and before we knew it, Gary Baker was on the line, ready to talk about having a sit-down meeting.

Now that the door was opened, Bob and Peter turned to me for help with a sales pitch. I still have the presentation I prepared. It's definitely one for the memory box. Our pitch was a little awkward, given Connolly had absolutely no healthcare experience to speak of. Instead, I decided it would be best if we explained how a recovery audit would work and served up as our credentials all of our Fortune 100 clients in other industries. The strategy did the trick, but none of us truly understood what could come from that meeting.

There was not much for us to lose, but if all went well, Connolly had everything to gain. Securing UnitedHealthcare as a client would mean breaking into an industry that our usual competitors had yet to tackle.

Sensing we were possibly on to something new, I called Larry to give him a heads-up. I needed him to know we had some guys going to a meeting to talk about a medical claims audit, a discussion we'd never had before. We needed him to be in the loop so we could prepare ourselves for what could come if we got the account.

Until then, Connolly had become accustomed to having our principals move independently. They knew that one of their main objectives was to go out and find new accounts. I believe that is the only thing that was on Peter Campisi's mind when he went after UnitedHealthcare, but it also meant some major changes for the rest of the business. Now that things were gaining traction and the meeting was really underway, we had to stop ourselves in our tracks as if to say, "You know what? *Maybe* this is a good time to run some of this by our CEO."

We were very used to people following the entrepreneurial spirit that yielded so much of our success. But we also had more than our fair share of failures or suboptimal results that came with some of the new client or new market experiments we bet on.

I could name scores of fliers we took—calculated risks, if you will—that never materialized the way we had initially hoped. Marching into healthcare was just another one to add to that list, but we knew right away that it was a major change. The risk—and potential—were much different from anything else Connolly had ever contemplated.

Well, as fate would have it, the meeting took place, and our team walked away with the assignment. We received our first set of files containing personal medical claim information, including sensitive data like Social Security numbers, and then it finally hit us.

We are really doing this!

The revelation was a mix of "Oh wow, this is interesting!" and "Oh crap, what do we do?" all at the same time.

UnitedHealthcare in 1998 was not the same payer we know today. We joined forces with the company at the very beginning of its evolution. One of the things I love most about this story is the fact that they are *still* a Connolly client today. Although the initial relationship was an impromptu leap of faith, we rose to the challenge and proved our value, offering us the privilege of growing alongside them for now twenty-plus years.

FACED WITH A CHALLENGING CLIMATE

Our timing couldn't have been better. Connolly segued into health-care when the industry itself was being inundated with change and expansion. Back then, the nation expressed a keen interest in restructuring our healthcare system, with a specific focus on how health insurance organizations worked.

During the late 1990s, there was a lot of backlash toward the original blueprint for health maintenance organizations (HMOs), which were initiated by the federal HMO Act of 1973. HMOs were an attempt to solve the tremendous problem of skyrocketing healthcare costs, but they were not without flaws.

The idea was simple: control costs by requiring healthcare consumers to use only those doctors within a network approved by the insurer. In exchange for the constant flow of patients, doctors agreed to only bill the insurer a predetermined fee. Consumers benefited by paying fixed fees for healthcare with out-of-pocket expenses limited to a specified co-pay, but people were not used to choosing a doctor from a list provided by an insurance company. Also, healthcare providers (hospitals and doctors) were confused by a system that required them to bill the insurer rather than the patient. As might be expected, confusion reigned for both consumers and doctors, which did very little for the success of the HMO movement.

Eventually, President Bill Clinton asked his wife, Hillary, to head a task force to help circumvent these issues, which helped HMOs unravel into the system we're familiar with today: one plan, one price for in-network treatment, and one price for out-of-network providers. Some plans go the extra mile to extend a variety of options to the insured, but these changes did not take effect without a considerable amount of trial and error.

It wasn't all bad for commercial health insurers. With the exception of a short period of time in the early '90s, overall spending on healthcare in the US was substantial at 13.4 percent of GDP in 2000, up from 12.1 percent in 1990 and heading to 17.3 percent or $2.6 trillion by 2010 and $3.65 trillion in 2018. This growth has been fueled by several factors, not the least of which is the aging of baby boomers. As they grow older, the demand for expensive medical procedures has grown as well. Chronic illnesses such as diabetes and heart disease have also been on the rise. And legislation like the 2003 Medicare Modernization Act shifted even more opportunity to commercial payers with the establishment of Medicare Advantage and Medicare Part D (prescriptions), which tripled the number of people using those plans.

Where you once had a simple system of paying for a visit to the doctor or hospital, the quagmire of medical claims processing that grew out of the forays into HMOs, managed care, Medicare, Medicare Advantage, Medicaid, and managed Medicaid created an immense opportunity for errors to occur. Claim payment policies are constantly changing, complicating an already challenging payment environment. All of this created a very rich opportunity to find errors, which ranged from 6 percent in the commercial (non-government) healthcare sector to 10–12 percent for Medicare and Medicaid. This meant that overpayments in the healthcare market were in excess of $220 billion in 2018. In comparison, we saw error rates in the retail sector of less than one tenth of 1 percent.

With the opportunity in healthcare being driven by these macrolevel dynamics, the market we were entering was rife with competition. There were other, larger recovery audit firms like HMS, Accent, AIM, and Rawlings, who not only had a head start but were singularly focused on servicing the healthcare sector. These firms were chock full of healthcare professionals, and they did not have the same competing priorities that we had at Connolly, such as resourcing our other divisions (retail, commercial, and international). Beyond all the external competitors, most of our clients had internal recovery teams focused on finding improper payments ahead of us.

Although we entered the healthcare business with high expectations of a ripe opportunity, the more we learned about the industry, the more we recognized the need to leave our rose-colored glasses behind. Before long, it became clear to us that healthcare was set to be a cutthroat market, one that would call for us to work harder than ever before if we were to move ahead of our competition and become the primary outsourced vendor of choice.

Let's just say our clients really made us work to earn our position. At one point, UnitedHealthcare simply released their data simultaneously to all outside vendors, making it a race among competitors to tag their improper payments and demonstrate whose technology and algorithms were the most effective. Time and again, Connolly was forced to step up to these types of client challenges, and each time, we excelled. I believe these difficult, competitive client situations forced us to rise to the occasion and deliver superior results. Ultimately, the competition made us a better company and helped us prove that we were true leaders in the field.

RECRUITING FOR A NEW DIVISION

Even with the "happily ever after" ending, our start in the healthcare industry was anything but a fairy tale. It took a lot of effort and tenacity for us to get as far as we did. The challenges we faced were considerable, and we were not exactly equipped with all we needed to manage them.

Aside from the foundational issues presented by the marketplace, one of our most difficult obstacles was trying to understand how to audit medical claims using the legacy systems UnitedHealthcare had in place at the time. When it came to assigning staff to the job, we had to accept the fact that, even with all our experience, we did not have a pool of healthcare-savvy auditors to recruit from. The only solution was persuading some of our Atlanta-based auditors to take on the assignment and training talent from the ground up.

With so much on the line, I worked alongside Peter Campisi to develop the best approach. The first order of business was to deploy Robert, who personally stepped up to handle the data and tool-set development for the account start-up. It was completely new; there were a number of risks involved, and his instincts told him not to delegate until we had a feel for what we were dealing with.

Robert didn't see the need for removing talent from other assignments that were already productive, just to have them take a dive into healthcare, especially since we were not even sure we would be successful in this new market. Bear in mind, the only background we had on the industry came from our talks with Peter and the articles we read in the press surrounding the managed-care revolution. We recognized the potential, but we also noticed the risk of exposure and the liabilities that came with mishandling personal health information—which meant government fines, big fines! So rather than disrupt the team in Stamford, who was busy with existing retail and commercial accounts, Robert, in true Rob fashion, said, "I'll take this one on."

Of course, the simplicity of his response to my request does not fully capture just how much we benefited from Robert's willingness to step up to lead us in a new direction. When we got our first set of data files from UnitedHealthcare, Robert jumped right in with both feet. During those first few months, we all put in our best effort to let our resounding "figure it out" mentality take the lead.

With Larry's help, we accumulated a team of seasoned Connolly auditors, who he convinced to take on a risky assignment in unchartered waters, and started by adopting some of our basic algorithms—duplicate payments. It worked! We found lots of them. With this preliminary research under our belts, we knew we were onto something.

I could say "and the rest was history," but there is so much more to this story. In the beginning, it took forever to get the division off the ground. Peter, Robert, and I were making headway in terms of people and processes. Peter Campisi helped us open the door. I coordinated with Larry to make sure we were resourced and to get our affairs in order. Robert took on the challenge of helping us sort through the maze that was the client's data-processing system. From soup to nuts, we were gearing up to take on a considerable shift in our business.

After some thought, we realized that we were still missing one major component, something that could help us succeed by establishing our goals and helping us build out our ideas. What we were missing was a leader.

I was already managing multiple segments of Connolly at the time, and Larry had his plate full as CEO. Together, we knew that the build-out of healthcare would require the oversight of someone who could give it their undivided attention. Then the perfect candidate came to mind.

In October 1998, Larry approached our cousin, Mike Sick, at a family funeral, with a unique proposition. The passing of our uncle Tom Tinsley created the setting for an unlikely offer. Mike did not know how serious Larry was at the time, but he was offered a position with Connolly on the spot.

Larry knew Mike had history working with Oxford Health in New York while they created their Medicare Advantage program, a business started in 1992 to sell insurance to seniors over sixty-five.[18]

---

18   https://www.oxhp.com/oxford_medicare_advantage/html/doma_aoma.html

Mike ran the sales and marketing aspect of the project, creating pitches to sell the product to their target audience.

Initially, Oxford's Medicare Advantage was a major success, and the company signed on a ton of customers. Before long, the health plan experienced the same problem many others faced in this industry. Oxford struggled to identify the difference between paid and outstanding claims. There was a lot of money being circulated, but they had difficulty differentiating which claims had been paid and which were still outstanding.

Enrolling such a large number of new Medicare beneficiaries possibly ended up becoming Oxford's downfall. They grew larger than they could manage, and the company was experiencing major IT issues. Eventually, their stock plunged, leading UnitedHealthcare to sweep in and buy the company.

After walking away from his position with Oxford, Mike returned to Johnson & Johnson, a company into which he'd previously invested twenty years. His resume proved that Mike had experienced the highs and lows of healthcare firsthand. It also convinced him that he was no longer interested in entertaining the colorless advantages of working in corporate America. All of which made him the perfect candidate for what we were building at Connolly.

When Larry made his first offer to Mike, the healthcare opportunity was not initially presented. We just knew Mike had the qualities and experience that could help us grow. Initially, Mike was offered his pick of a few positions. Negotiations took about a year of exchanges, since accepting the idea of being paid on contingency and the unpredictable nature of our industry were a lot for Mike to consider.

Finally, Larry was prepared to come to the table with a strong offer, but to our surprise, Mike was no longer interested. He got wind of discussions we were having with General Electric, who was interested in buying out Connolly. For Mike, the idea of working under another *Fortune* 500 company left a sour taste in his mouth. Connolly's entrepreneurial nature was what had first caught his attention. Mike was not interested in the idea of going down the corporate route again.

About six months later, Larry resurfaced, this time with good news. The GE deal had fallen through. Connolly was too small, and they rescinded their offer. Just like that, Mike was all ears.

It could not have happened at a more perfect time. Over the course of that year, we broke into the surprisingly lucrative healthcare industry, and at the rate we were growing, Mike's experience made him the ideal person to become the president of our healthcare division.

It just made sense. Even with the combined skills and expertise of the initial group of folks we put on our first few assignments, all of us were operating on a string of educated guesses. Larry and I did not have a clear understanding of how to make the most of this opportunity, and more importantly, neither of us had the bandwidth to give healthcare our undivided attention. Simultaneously, we were focused on building up the known success we were having in the UK and the US retail and commercial markets, as well as our IC-to-EE transition. Mike was the missing piece that could help us keep this opportunity on the table.

Once we laid the framework, we needed our new healthcare president to open more doors. With his background in sales and marketing, he knew what it took to get major clients to sit down and have a meeting with us. We were already predisposed to a tall-building strategy, knowing from experience it can take as much effort to land a whale as it does a minnow. Considering the potential posed by the healthcare sector, we wanted to concentrate our attention on the biggest fish in the sea, and Mike was eager to help us attempt to reel them in.

I came to Connolly in 1999, the year after the first pilot program was developed. My job was to "go out and get clients." From the very beginning, Connolly went after tall buildings—and by that, I mean the "big boys," the major healthcare payers. Not easy when you have no track record and the market doesn't understand your business.

—*Mike Sick*

I spoke with Mike in preparation for this book because, of all the things we could point out, all the stories we could tell about this whirlwind experience, I had one pressing question for him. Why? Why leave behind the security of an executive position to take this wildly undefined adventure with us?

He said, "They say you should never take a job because you're running away from one, but I was tired of big company culture." To him, the fact that Connolly was new and different from anything he'd ever experienced was actually attractive.

Yes, the position presented its fair share of risks, but Mike noticed the success Connolly was having. He was confident in our ability to re-create that momentum in healthcare. Overall, Mike shared a lot of our beliefs, and he was not afraid of taking his shot. He was perfect for us.

I will say, it did not take long before he got a glimpse of some of the challenges that can make our industry so draining. Success for Connolly did not take place overnight. We experienced some of the same trial and error while establishing ourselves in healthcare.

When I spoke with him, Mike described the experience as a

"fairly brutal first three to three and a half years," and I would not disagree. Signing on Mike meant that we could finally have someone dedicated to helping Connolly grow beyond the groundwork we'd laid at our first assignment. Connolly had placed an incredible amount of emphasis on the UnitedHealthcare account. We needed that engagement to succeed so we could expand from there and hand over a story to Mike that he could market to other prospective clients.

Let's just say that, in business, you must always be equipped with a backup plan.

GROWTH THROUGH OPPORTUNITY

We don't know what we don't know. Since neither Mike nor I truly had a healthcare background, that was the approach that carried us through this adventure. From the beginning, we were realistic about our shortcomings and committed to learning as much as we could. We studied the issues and payment structures that were native to healthcare. Until we brought our understanding up to speed, we concentrated on the very basics, things Connolly understood, like duplicate payments and contract compliance. Since talent was scarce, we transferred over a few of our veteran auditors from Atlanta, like Terry Tankersley, Patrick Knight, and Evelyn Ball, for the first assignment, hoping their experience would help us navigate our way. Interestingly enough, that first round of audits kind of ended up as a turkey shoot. We actually found a lot of errors—and money!

From the beginning, we were realistic about our shortcomings and committed to learning as much as we could.

The client took notice, and next we were invited to take a look at a few other UnitedHealthcare divisions. As it turns out, Gary Baker, our CFO client for UHC's Alabama division, was connected with the head of finance at the Chicago division too. He put in the good word and helped us land another assignment with them.

One by one, we expanded into various UnitedHealthcare divisions. Eventually, UHC centralized all these small regional plans, but back then, we had to start from scratch each time we ventured into a new division. You would think it would be simple to move from one division to another, especially since we were working within the same company, but at the time, each of these divisions ran their units independently. All of their payment systems were different, which meant more for Connolly to decipher. Each CFO was also responsible for their own P&L—great news for us, since they were looking for our help to improve their profitability. But relearning each business unit was a painstaking process.

Nevertheless, Connolly performed consistently. We were building experience and finding new sources of financial "leakage"—errors.

Our findings were adding up. We thought things were heading in the right direction, but we were unaware that there was still a major part of the process missing from the equation.

While we were expanding our footprint region by region, within the different divisions of UnitedHealthcare, the client had been on a buying spree and was busy integrating all of the regional payers they acquired and centralizing the redundant operations that resided in each of the divisions, including claims processing. Connolly was having a lot of success finding improper payments, but processing offsets in all these disparate systems proved to be a much more complex transaction that could only be done manually.

Despite the regional differences, all of UnitedHealthcare's claims systems were designed primarily to process claims and *pay* one way.

Their systems were rudimentary, primarily structured to adjudicate and pay claims. Initially, the margin for error wasn't a prioritized consideration. When Connolly stepped in and identified a slew of duplicate payments and other oversights, we had no clue that UnitedHealthcare would become restricted by a major systems issue that made reconciling those payments difficult.

With such a basic payment system, the client could not efficiently *recover* the overages we discovered by offset. The entire process was designed to be payment focused and didn't contemplate adjustments. As a result of our reviews, a substantial amount of improper payments was identified. We were paid millions based on our contingency fee, but the highlight of our economic fee-sharing model was not being realized since UnitedHealthcare was unable to recover the overpayments we identified.

Plain and simple, they had no automated way get their money back.

The overpayments Connolly identified highlighted a major wrinkle. The concept of taking money back from a provider via offset, while efficient, was new. Until we came into the equation, providers would submit a claim, and they were simply reimbursed for it, or the claim was denied. The idea of a provider being reimbursed for an inaccurate claim that would later be adjusted was foreign. Instead, those types of transaction adjustments would be handled typically by a reimbursement check. This created an environment where all these checks were going back and forth, requiring a

> *The overpayments Connolly identified highlighted a major wrinkle. The concept of taking money back from a provider via offset, while efficient, was new.*

lot of incremental administrative effort and time for both the providers and payers.

Before we stepped in, payers weren't focused on accuracy issues and weren't considering the idea that claims might not be priced or coded correctly. Our work shed light on a major pain point that forced UnitedHealthcare to start performing patchwork on their systems. It was a massive task, but the client was more than willing to make the investment because it was clear that the losses were substantial. We're talking millions and millions of dollars left on the table. Even with all they were recovering on their own, we shed light on an issue that could not, in good conscience, be ignored.

Connolly was working across multiple divisions while United-Healthcare was struggling to solve some major integration issues. To top things off, the company rebranded as UnitedHealth Group (UHG) around the same time, creating two distinct platforms, UnitedHealthcare and Optum, and continued their path of acquiring regional payers, insurance companies, and healthcare IT capabilities, adding topline expansion as the icing on the cake.

With so many variables to consider, we had to plan our steps appropriately and did so by taking small measures until we mastered the process and cracked the code. In doing so, we put ourselves in the position to learn. These discoveries helped us strategize while we prepared for what we hoped would be continual expansion.

A CASH-OUT CRISIS

Even with the systems issues, we thought we were making great progress. Connolly was performing as promised. We even shadowed with a few of the regional payers to help them identify ways to make their systems more adaptable. Then everything came to a halt.

In January 2000, only about a year after Mike Sick joined the business, we found out that we were at risk of losing our only health-care client. Representatives for UnitedHealth Group corporate, the big guns, requested a meeting with us at their Chicago offices, a meeting neither Mike Sick nor I will ever forget.

After a cordial lunch, the tone changed dramatically, and we quickly found out that they were furious about the backlogs we had created and the lack of progress they were making to modify their systems. From our perspective, we had invested months of work and expenses, with the promise that the system fixes were imminent. Meanwhile, they had been paying us according to our agreement, which actually furthered their financial exposure, as they had yet to get their systems working and collect on the debts we discovered. Though the issue was no fault of ours, the client was understandably upset. With no one else to take the brunt of their fury, they took us to the woodshed and wanted us to help make things right.

Their demand was set to the tune of about $2 million. They basically sat us down and said, "We paid you this money, and you were only supposed to benefit if we did. We haven't, so we want our money back."

Talk about a blow to the gut.

Getting fired from UnitedHealth Group, our first ever health-care client, would ruin us! Losing that assignment would sacrifice the foothold we'd gained in the entire sector. All our work, our reputation, and our future in the healthcare sector were at stake. Not to mention the panic of coming up with $2 million, which was a tremendous amount of money to us back then. We were over our ski tips.

The client was screaming. Tension was thick. Everything we had planned was officially at risk.

How do you deal with a client suddenly demanding that you

repay millions of dollars that you do not have to give?

How do you respond when your client is glaring at you, asking, "How come you didn't know this is where we would end up?"—especially when I was asking myself the same question!

We were learning the hard way that the healthcare industry was not as primed as the retail sector to handle the volume of transactions our work generated. Connolly had been working for retailers for twenty years. We knew that industry and their payment systems inside and out. Strict rules and regulations topped by rudimentary healthcare payment systems yielded minimal access and visibility. Essentially, we were trying to learn how to master a market that we could only partially see.

Our client's finance department was signing off on our invoices, so we thought all was in order. Maybe there was something more that we could have done, but it seemed like our hands were tied. We weren't managing the IT resources that were modifying their payment systems. Each time we revealed a new way to improve their system, we hit a brick wall. Our only option was to support the notion of doing the work around the blockages and devising a way to quantify the financial benefits of keeping us aboard.

Our client was literally bleeding money. That we knew for sure. Leaving that dreary January meeting, Mike and I were feeling ice cold walking down Michigan Avenue. It was winter in Chicago, but the chill we shared had little to do with the elements.

For me, this was a real "holy crap" moment. I looked at Mike and thought about all he had put at risk to join our business, and I assumed he would be in a panic. It was less than a year after he signed on, and we were on the brink of losing our one and only healthcare client. I called Larry and hailed Mayday, but Mike was cool, calm, and collected. I said, "Mike, we are about to get fired, we can't get fired!" He looked at me and said, "I'll get this fixed, Libby. Don't worry about it."

And he did.

It seemed impossible, but somehow, Mike managed to smooth things over with our client. The uproar kind of reminded me of the Channel account situation we dealt with years prior. It was another case of our discovering a major system flaw and too much money.

We were being penalized for discovering errors that exceeded our client's ability to recover. Because they paid us, it was a direct contradiction to our original agreement and indirectly broke our promise to guarantee that our client received an economic benefit from our services. In the end, we realized that the client was suffering because of that tremendous processing backlog we created.

They desperately needed to update their systems to allow for claims adjustments, whether identified by us, them, or anyone else. They also recognized that they needed to make organizational investments and promoted Bob Starman to vice president of vendor management and appeals. Bob's job was to create a centralized recovery and appeal function for United. He was talented and fair. The financial reality was that they needed to collect those improper payments just as much as we needed them to collect.

To save this relationship, Connolly resurrected our old consulting ways and worked side by side with UnitedHealthcare to help them sort through the mess. This is where Robert's influence really came in to help. He leveraged the know-how of his IT team to guide us through this technological storm. Temporarily, Connolly had to use our own resources to create a work-around while the client

To save this relationship, Connolly resurrected our old consulting ways and worked side by side with UnitedHealthcare to help them sort through the mess.

was working on a more permanent fix.

Think about it: the client *wanted* to see the results. They also wanted us around because, if their regional finance division leaders could successfully recover the money we found, it would make their profitability look better and boost earnings. We were not going to let this relationship end on a sour note, especially without proving that Connolly could do exactly what we promised to do. We came there to do a job, and we would not leave until that job was done correctly. So we pooled our talent and went all in.

The process was a bit tenuous for a while, but we pushed through. Increasing our involvement with UnitedHealthcare's systems issues helped us realize just how significant the opportunity was. It proved that healthcare was an industry that could change the scope of our business forever.

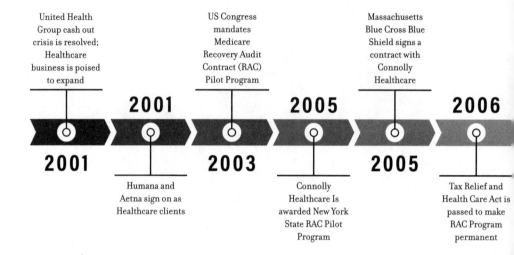

United Health Group cash out crisis is resolved; Healthcare business is poised to expand

2001

US Congress mandates Medicare Recovery Audit Contract (RAC) Pilot Program

2005

Massachusetts Blue Cross Blue Shield signs a contract with Connolly Healthcare

2006

2001

Humana and Aetna sign on as Healthcare clients

2003

Connolly Healthcare Is awarded New York State RAC Pilot Program

2005

Tax Relief and Health Care Act is passed to make RAC Program permanent

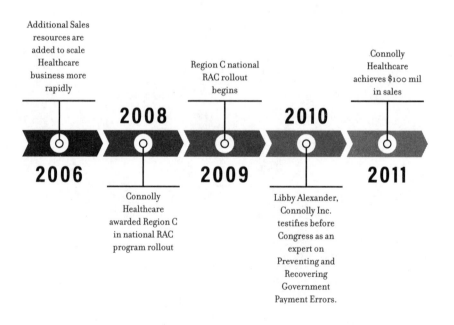

Additional Sales resources are added to scale Healthcare business more rapidly

2008

Region C national RAC rollout begins

2010

Connolly Healthcare achieves $100 mil in sales

2006

Connolly Healthcare awarded Region C in national RAC program rollout

2009

Libby Alexander, Connolly Inc. testifies before Congress as an expert on Preventing and Recovering Government Payment Errors.

2011

CHAPTER 8

Quantifiable Proof

Expanding Our Efforts After
Success in Healthcare

One of the reasons I think I have been successful is that I try to have an
open mind. It's important to realize that you don't know what you don't
know, and be willing to work on it. Self-awareness is really important.

—Libby Connolly Alexander

About a year after the crisis in Chicago, we finally got our work for UnitedHealthcare back on track. When we hired Mike in 1999, he was given one mission: to expand our healthcare business. Unfortunately, it took about three years for us to be sure that we could tackle this industry.

Our first few years were tangled in figuring out how to execute while helping UnitedHealthcare sort through their processing issues. It was something we had to do. I mean, it's kind of hard to get another client when you're on the verge of losing your one and only reference.

Before 2001, we were not in a position to expand. Eventually, we untangled the knots and finally got our narrative together. We were now working for three divisions: Alabama, Chicago, and Texas. With results in hand, it was time to work on securing our next client.

The next door to open was Humana. After multiple meetings, we were finally able to convince them to give us a pilot. We were confident and willing to take the risk. We knew we could demonstrate value if they just gave us a shot with their data.

"Let us prove it" was our fallback pitch. We had a strong track record, just not with healthcare payers. Our client roster was chock full of the largest retailers and manufacturers in the country. Even with all the blue-chip names, it did not mean a thing to potential healthcare clients. Despite all of our years of experience and the millions upon millions of dollars we had recovered since the company's inception, entering healthcare meant we had to reestablish ourselves in this new market. It wasn't easy.

Each time we landed a new client meant we had to gear up for execution. We usually handled it by moving folks around, taking experienced talent from one client and assigning it to the next. Only in this case, we didn't have experience to reassign. We needed a team to handle the Humana account, and we had nobody in Louisville. It was time to start hiring.

We also knew we needed more healthcare expertise. Naturally, we started hunting for people with backgrounds in the industry, people with claims payment experience or experience in healthcare claim operations. It seemed logical at the time. Everyone had more knowledge than Mike and I; we knew that too. All we were after was the chance to pick their brains.

Our plan was to learn what they knew so we could pair our payment integrity experience with their healthcare expertise. We were never above saying, "Hey, you know more about healthcare than we do. Come help us!" It was a winning attitude. It was also that open mind that led us to the first assignment in Alabama to begin with. In fact, we strategically maintained that same open-ended town hall approach for as long as I was involved with the company. It is well understood that culture is defined at the top. Since neither Mike nor I had background in healthcare, we were of the opinion that everyone knew more than we did, so we did a lot of listening. This created an environment of humility and openness that helped shape and fuel our growth. The beauty of the entire model was that there was an impressive financial incentive backing this culture that left everyone motivated to help us figure it out. We didn't say yes to everything, but our desire to learn, to become the best at what we did, certainly helped us decide what we would say yes to.

> *We were of the opinion that everyone knew more than we did, so we did a lot of listening. This created an environment of humility and openness that helped shape and fuel our growth.*

We were especially incentivized to help our frontline people. It was never about titles or egos; we were focused on results. Our auditors knew that they couldn't make money if we didn't support them in every way possible. If it took people like me, those sitting at the top of the proverbial totem pole, to stand at the front of the pack and say, "What's the best way to do this?" then no one else had any issue with making suggestions.

I believe it was this level of openness that turned Connolly Healthcare into such a formidable team. When it came to merging specialties and expertise, none of us had more or less hubris than the other. Mike and I were committed to using our curiosity as a propellant for change.

To kickstart his recruiting efforts, Mike created a very clever want ad that he would run in the newspaper. Yes, in the beginning, we recruited top talent through creative newspaper ads over and over again, a foreign concept that is rarely seen in today's world of online recruiting. Now we rely on platforms like Indeed or LinkedIn to give us a glimpse into a candidate's professional profile. Prospective talent has tools like Glassdoor to help them gather an idea of what the salary and culture are like at a company before submitting their resume. In the ancient days of hiring, we had newspapers.

You'd squeeze as much information as you could into a small ad, sometimes with nothing more than a sentence or two to help you attract qualified candidates. The digital revolution destroyed the need for newspaper advertising, but it was a treasured resource back in those days. Connolly chose to get creative with our limited recruitment space. Our ads would say something like:

Leading Global
Recovery Audit Firm
Looking for Healthcare
Industry Knowledge.

If you are clever and
like to solve puzzles,
we have a rewarding
career for you.

We recruited some of our most talented and longest-tenured associates through those wacky job advertisements, folks like Chad Janak, Mike McGauley, Lori Aronson, Rick McLaughlin, and Jeremy Bamford, just to name a few.

On one hand, we discovered a market segment that was growing rapidly. On the other, there was a lot of ground for us to cover, namely in the payment integrity sector. Healthcare payment integrity presented a new market for Connolly. We were well versed in searching for retail-specific errors, but advancing through healthcare meant we would need to develop the expertise to identify whether processed claims were paid correctly. This meant verifying that the appropriate party paid the claim, and in response for eligible members who received care according to their plan's contractual terms. Somehow we had to figure out how to get this done without violating HIPAA. To be frank, there were plenty of firms who already knew this space better than we did, businesses solely dedicated to the healthcare payment integrity space that already had relationships with the payers with whom we wanted to work.

Still, we figured it out.

We stayed outcome focused while recruiting experienced talent and feeling our way through the marketplace. We believed in the value we could deliver, and we remained results driven throughout the evolution of Connolly Healthcare. More importantly, we needed to do it in a way that would differentiate Connolly from our healthcare-specific competitors, including the payers' in-house departments. We had to figure it out, and if we were going to maintain the traction we had built by gaining those first major accounts, we needed to continue to recruit associates who had experience we didn't have.

Our retail experience taught us that every client is unique, so we continued to forge forward, investing and staffing around each opportunity. Our culture was built to welcome challenges and push our team's expertise to the limits. Even though we recognized that the healthcare space was far from Blue Ocean, we believed in our ability to execute. Connolly always remembered the principles that had brought us success. We stayed client focused, maintained low noise, and were results driven.

Using these proven strategies, we cultivated long-term relationships with these major payers, and in the end, we were rewarded with an average annual healthcare revenue growth rate in the 40 percent range, which Connolly maintained for well over ten years. It was one heck of an uphill battle, but the results say it all.

HEALTHCARE HAS BECOME A PRIMARY GROWTH ENGINE
Connolly annual revenue

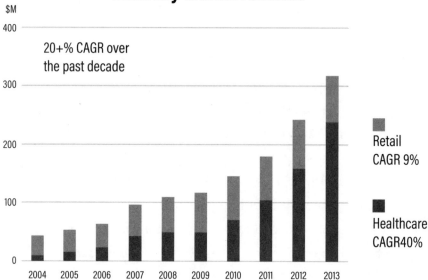

Market share with our clients increased. When we finally got Humana to agree to bring us on in 2001, we knew we were onto something special. Like many of the payers we contacted, at first,

Humana was skeptical about our services. They already had a sophisticated in-house recovery group producing significant results and were working with other recovery vendors. However, with the numbers we were creating at UnitedHealthcare, Humana could not help but consider the potential benefits of giving us a trial assignment.

Harold Davis, who ran Humana's internal recovery team, and his wife, Jan, who at the time also worked for Humana, were finally open to entertaining our proposal. It took fourteen months and more than a few trips to Louisville to reach that point. Mike and I traveled to meet Harold and Jan several times to discuss our capabilities and approach, but they got it. In the end, they took us up on our pilot offer. Humana's plan was to learn from us so they could bolster their internal team's expertise and results by absorbing our recovery audit experience. We accepted the challenge without hesitation.

Initially, it was curiosity that drove them to engage with us, but after our initial pilot in Jacksonville, the results were what kept us around. The more success we saw with other payers, the more Humana would question what they were missing themselves, which led us to scope increases. We were never worried about their internal function adopting and re-creating our work plan to build their own capacity—well, maybe a little bit. It was ambitious, to say the least, but they saw our value as twofold. One, the financial results we produced were too good to bypass. Two, our expertise allowed them to study the way we worked to build their own capabilities. This thought pattern was repeated client after client, each one realizing the multifaceted benefits of partnering with us. This is how they looked at Connolly's value proposition: we brought them industry insight and money they needed to recover, and they got to learn from us.

In 2001, more than three years after securing our first healthcare client, our sales cycle finally paid off. Shortly after signing our agreement with Humana, Aetna contracted with us as well. All of a sudden, we had three healthcare clients who also happened to be three of the largest commercial payers in the United States. With these big clients secured, now it was all about execution.

THE RISE OF CONNOLLY HEALTHCARE

With UHC, Humana, and Aetna on our roster, Connolly was tasked with really fortifying our talent pool. We had to work even harder to move beyond the "we don't know what we don't know" handicap; the time had come for us to focus our efforts. Not only did we have to figure it out, we had to continuously produce. Sure, we only had three accounts at the time, but those clients happened to be three of the biggest payers in the United States of America.

We stuck to perfecting our approach with those payers for the next few years. By 2005, Connolly was finally ready to accept a new contract, this time with our first Blue plan, Blue Cross Blue Shield of Massachusetts.

As far as execution, everything remained the same. Connolly Healthcare was devoted to settling ourselves in this industry. We were being pulled in so many directions. We spent these first few years defining our best practices, dealing with data, refining our algorithms and tool sets, and, of course, finding new sources of leakage. We were always hiring, always training, and always working to figure out what was best for us, our employees, and, of course, our clients.

Throughout our early foray into the healthcare market, we were careful not to tip our hand to competitors as to what we were doing and how successful we were. I referred to this as our submarine strategy. We never discussed our plans on the open market about how we were tackling the healthcare market. We did not need to brag about our accomplishments and disclose to the competition what we were doing. We knew what we were developing behind the scenes, and our clients offered the only validation we needed.

If we spoke about our growth too soon, we would have risked giving PRG and others space to use their resources to steal that opportunity away from us. Healthcare was rich territory, and we wanted to be certain that CCA had the runway to capture as much market share as possible. We had to be cautious and calculating while we measured each step and continued to plan the future of our business.

Then it happened: we got another major break.

The results we'd created from those other clients began to translate into potential for even larger assignments. No sooner had we begun to get comfortable with our approach to the payment integrity space than we stumbled upon an opportunity to bid on a recovery audit pilot program for Medicare.

Mike was always busy working on identifying new opportunities. Connolly had explored the idea of partnering with the federal government in the past but with little success. Luckily for us, Congress saw things differently and recognized the potential value of recovery auditing and applying a successful private sector practice to the government. In 2003, it mandated that the Centers for Medicare and Medicaid Services (CMS) perform a pilot program to determine if recovery audit contractors, RACs, could efficiently and effectively identify and recover improper payments for the Medicare Fee-for-Service (FFS) program. Errors were endemic to Medicare at this time (and continue to be!), with "improper payments" in the tens of billions of dollars annually. Finding even a small fraction of those errors could mean millions of dollars of revenue to Connolly.

Everybody in the business wanted to work on the CMS pilot. If Connolly could claim a space on the roster, that would open the door for us with other commercial payers. Even though we knew nothing about the Medicare Fee-for-Service program, Mike wanted to bid, and I trusted his instincts. "Libby, it's just too big to pass up," he said. We already had a lot on our plate, and we could have taken a pass, but we didn't. We continued to push the envelope, devoted to figuring it out along the way.

A ROUND WITH THE FEDERAL GOVERNMENT

Healthcare was finally working for us. With so much money recovered through our commercial insurance clients, we could not help but consider the opportunity that awaited us in the federal healthcare business, with its tremendous size and error rate. We tossed around the idea of moving into government contracts long before we broke into healthcare. Initially, we were eyeing any government agency as an opportunity.

Our competitors had the same idea. PRG was making investments and had dedicated resources to working the government market, again from a different vantage. I can remember when Paul Dinkins, a representative from PRG, testified before Congress in 1999 about how the government could benefit from our industry. This opened the door to a conversation on best practices.

The federal government was not as motivated to discover and recover over-payments as private sector, for-profit companies.

As attractive as the idea seemed, we later learned through experiences at the Department of Education and Department of Defense that the federal government was not as motivated to discover and recover overpayments as private sector, for-profit companies. All we did was hit brick walls. It didn't take long for us to realize that, if you go to the government and say, "Here are all the mistakes you made," they will usually write them off, claiming they would rather fix the problem on their own. Federal officials were more concerned with the optics of making errors than correcting them.

Still, the seed was planted, and eventually, it bore fruit. PRG did an excellent job of holding onto the ear of Congress, making the case for adopting a private sector best practice to address waste by saying, "But why *wouldn't* you want to do this?" Congress finally agreed and passed the Improper Payments Information Act in 2002. But it was the Medicare Modernization Act passed in 2003 that authorized the three-year pilot program for Medicare FFS. CMS issued an RFP that not only narrowed the field of who could bid but also chose for the pilot the three largest Medicare FFS states in the country: California, New York, and Florida.

Kevin, our marketing executive, had already secured for us a General Services Administration (GSA) contract, a prerequisite to bidding. The stakes were high; everybody wanted to work on the CMS pilot. If Connolly could claim a space on the roster and execute on the contract, it could be enormously lucrative and set us up long term and potentially open up more doors with other commercial payers.

I can still remember the day Mike called to say we had won an award for the state of New York. It was March 2005, my oldest son, Aaron, and I were vacationing with Larry and his family in Colorado at Vail. We had just finished a great day of skiing when Mike called to say, "Libby, we got a contract award. We are doing this." Larry and I were sitting with our kids at an outdoor fire pit, enjoying après ski. We had a toast to celebrate, but all I could think was that we knew absolutely nothing about Medicare and would somehow have to figure it out.

Until that point, our health-care experience was strictly with commercial payers and insurers. We signed UnitedHealthcare in 1998, Humana and Aetna in 2001, then Blue Cross Blue Shield in 2005. We had absolutely no history with coding reviews and had never audited a medical chart.

All I could think was that we knew absolutely nothing about Medicare and would somehow have to figure it out.

We didn't know it at the time, but that was what this CMS audit would be all about. If we had used our lack of experience as an excuse to bypass the opportunity, we would have never gotten into coding or medical necessity reviews, which are now a substantial part of the company's business revenue today. Even without any experience, this opportunity forced us to learn how to do what was required of us. That willingness to figure it out created a substantial future line of business and value for Connolly Healthcare.

Things got off on a slow start, but eventually, the pilot was a huge success.

Congress and Medicare officials could not ignore the results the pilot program created. The Tax Relief and Health Care Act of 2006 made the program permanent. Congress mandated that the program be rolled out nationally, and CMS split the country into four regions. Before long, the new contract returned $100 million in revenue to Connolly in just one year. To date, the Recovery Audit Contractor, or RAC, program as a whole has returned more than $10 billion to the Medicare trust fund. Our initial efforts helped to extend the life of the program by two full years. We *really* had the government's attention then, but we also drew the ire of the country's biggest lobbyist: the American Hospital Association.

Amid the success of the RAC program, hospitals began lobbying intensely to stop our work. Given that hospitals are typically the largest employer in any given congressperson's district, the AHA had willing ears with their narrative on how the "RACs," as they called us, were disrupting the way they were reimbursed and even going so far as to question how a doctor should treat his or her patients. Given their clout, over time the AHA virtually shut down the program. Despite the Medicare FFS program's roughly $45 billion in annual waste, today RACs are restricted to reviewing just .5 percent of a hospital's claims, which stands in stark contrast to the commercial payers, where virtually all claims are reviewed[19].

ACCELERATING GROWTH

Becoming a RAC meant our days of running in stealth mode were over. Everything about Medicare's program was public, including our results and even our rates. Our "submarine" had surfaced.

Everyone in the payer business looked at CMS as the big gorilla. After all, at over $700 billion in spend and growing, no one processes more claims than Medicare, and many systems, reimbursement policies and coding practices emanated from them. Whatever they did, everyone else followed suit[20].

Having CMS as a client was in many ways a seal of approval. Add on top that we had three of the largest commercial healthcare payers in the country as clients, and all of sudden Connolly was a leader, if not *the* leader, of healthcare recovery auditing in the country. Did

---

19   This data is based on Connolly industry experience working with the majority of the top twenty-five US healthcare payers.

20   Health and Human Services, HHS FY 2018 Budget in Brief, "CMS—Medicare." HHS.gov.

this mean we could rest on our laurels? No. In fact the pressure was on us more than ever to perform. All of our results were reported by CMS directly to Congress, which was even more reason for us to dedicate our efforts to coming out on top.

Interestingly, PRG was also one of the three recovery audit firms selected for the initial demonstration project. Although they essentially knew nothing about auditing healthcare, they were well versed in the government's contracting game, which led to them winning a contract. In fact, when we bid the Department of Defense contract, PRG was the company that won against us, because on paper, they had better "federal experience." They managed to win one of the Medicare demonstration contracts without *any* commercial healthcare experience as well. Despite the head start we had in the commercial healthcare sector, we were suddenly very fearful PRG would gain a toehold in the healthcare market via the federal door that had just opened. One way to thwart them was to outperform their results, but we needed to do so without creating problems for the client. Not only were we able to do that, but PRG created problems with hospitals in its demo program state, California, which ultimately led to their failure to win a slice of the country when the national contracts were awarded. This effectively meant they were finished in the healthcare space and would ultimately exit the business entirely.

PRG has proven to be a resilient company, and to their credit, they did manage to make a go of it for a while. They figured out quickly that they needed to subcontract the work to a firm with expertise in medical claim coding and picked an excellent subcontractor. We also hired someone, partnering with a nurse from Brooklyn who had a dual sense of understanding. She came to the space with coding experience and medical knowledge, which directed her efforts to the right areas. The work she performed became a model for us as we expanded our Medicare operation after winning a region when the national contract was rolled out.

The pilot program was not only new but highly visible and sensitive with the provider community. We understood that to be successful, we were going to have to work hard in New York to gain the respect of providers for the work we were doing. This was a sophisticated and tough crowd, and we weren't always welcome, but we treaded carefully. There was a lot at risk. If one thing fell out of place, we could create a situation that might permanently damage our reputation. Ultimately, that's what shot PRG in the foot. Moving too aggressively, they unintentionally bankrupted a hospital and knocked themselves out of the running before establishing their credibility in the market.

With the success we were having with Medicare and our large commercial clients, you would think that prospective clients would be coming to *us* instead of the other way around. Certainly Mike Sick's job was made easier, but now that the list of potential payer clients he wanted to chase was much longer, he needed help. In 2006, we were finally ready to hire our first dedicated, experienced salesperson for healthcare, Neal Miller, who embarked on a campaign of acquiring new clients.

With Neal on board, one by one new clients started to roll in the door. That's not to say winning them was easy, but our reputation as a leader in the field was firmly established, and that certainly helped. Our excellent execution for existing clients also helped, as many of our current clients were more than willing to go to bat for us as a reference.

One of the highlights for me at this time was being asked to testify before Congress's Subcommittee on Federal Financial Management in 2010 while Senator Tom Carper of Delaware was chairman. Along with three other CEOs, I shared details of our industry, our work in the private sector, and the impact recovery auditing could have on the future of federal healthcare and federal spending in general. In many ways this was a validation that our industry provided a valuable service for reining in rising healthcare costs.

One of the highlights for me at this time was being asked to testify before Congress's Subcommittee on Federal Financial Management.

It took eight years, but with our credentials firmly established, we were finally positioned to scale our healthcare division more rapidly.

SHIFTING THE COMPANY'S FOCUS

Although our healthcare business was accelerating, the growth was not without its pain points. Scaling resources and infrastructure to support the growth was extremely challenging, as was integrating the division into our existing business.

The experience over time created highly "lumpy" revenue streams and an unpredictable business proposition—a nightmare for a business to manage, but it forced us to get creative. After the demonstration program and before the rollout of our national contract award for Region C, we experienced our first pause in work.

We had a team of highly experienced people I didn't want to lay off, which started a discussion on alternatives. Mike Sick and I, along with some of our other key leaders working on CMS, were discussing options when I turned to Mike and suggested we leverage our strong commercial relationships and approach a few clients about doing the same types of reviews for them that we were doing for CMS. It worked. Not only did it save our staff, but performing clinical chart reviews is now a core part of the company's revenue, and also one of the fastest growing. Like everything else we did at Connolly, we started slow, cracked the code, and then started scaling up. We built systems, developed software, and began working with emerging technologies like machine learning and AI that allowed us to receive, handle, distribute, and perform hundreds of thousands of medical chart reviews. Had it not been for our work with CMS, we would not have pursued this path. In 2008, performing clinical chart reviews for commercial payers was not on our radar. When one door shuts, another opens.

And healthcare wasn't the only part of the business experiencing growth between 2001 and 2010.

Our retail division, led by John Merrill, was having tremendous success winning primary business away from PRG, although this was tempered by rate pressure, and the growth horizon for this market segment was slowing.

Our commercial division, led by Bob Donahue, was also experiencing growth, albeit on a much smaller scale and was much less profitable. Two thousand seven was a milestone year, with Connolly reaching $100 million in revenue. Retail was still the leading contributor to that number, while healthcare was just slightly less but growing faster. It was an exciting moment for this company founded in 1979, so we took the opportunity to commemorate the achievement by flying 100-plus members of our management team and their spouses to a beachfront celebration in Puerto Rico. Our oldest brother, Jim Connolly, and his wife, Nancy, even came down to join the celebration as a surprise. Jim gave a touching speech and honored Larry and me with an achievement award. It was a special night. We celebrated, we danced, and we had fun!

Just four years later, our healthcare division would be celebrating its own achievement of reaching $100 million in revenue on its own, a more than 100 percent increase over the 2007 figure.

Even though it didn't take twenty-eight years like the rest of the business, this growth was not without challenge. Looking back, our Medicare contract was perhaps the most difficult client environment to manage. We worked on contingency, while the government was accustomed to fixed cost structures. Blindly, we approached this client relationship with the same strategies we used within our traditional commercial client relationships. The only difference was the government was motivated by entirely different incentives. They cared about being fair. Our business model was based on the bottom line. We were results driven, but the government had to appease many different groups of people. Our measures of success were dramatically different, and we had to adapt. We had to quickly scale up the account, hiring scores of nurses, certified medical coders, IT staff, administrators, and even a few medical directors, only to have to scale right back down when the client decided to pull back on the reins once they saw our results.

Washington's powerful American Hospital Association and American Medical Association lobbyists made it their agenda to halt the RAC program. They have been successful; the program has been all but gutted today.

Our work highlighted flaws in reimbursement policy as well as flaws in the way provider appeals were handled. This caused CMS to pause the program while they sorted things out. And Washington's powerful American Hospital Association and American Medical Association lobbyists made it their agenda to halt the RAC program.

They have been successful; the program has been all but gutted today.

Even though our healthcare business was growing rapidly, our legacy retail and commercial segments were still contributing tens of millions of dollars in revenue. As a company, we knew those markets well and were more comfortable talking about them. Healthcare was different and not as broadly understood within our own organization. The types of audits we were performing were different, and with that came a new vernacular to talk about them. Healthcare was the up-and-comer, with two key attractive drivers: more market opportunity and better margins. We would walk out of internal meetings and quarterly business reviews excited about the business, declare we should be spending more time talking about healthcare, and align resources accordingly, but we struggled to make the shift. Instead, we would defer focus on the challenges of our legacy divisions.

No matter how large we grew, it was imperative for us to maintain the integrity of the Connolly brand. But interdepartmental dissension and operational challenges were putting the principles that kept us going in previous years in jeopardy. The last thing we wanted was to go down in history as the company that got so big it capsized. We knew the business had more potential. We also knew that after thirty-plus years of our "figure it out" approach, we were struggling and needed help getting the business to the next level.

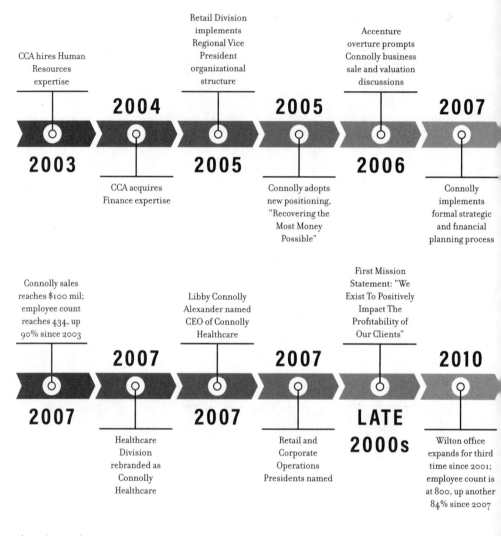

CCA hires Human Resources expertise

Retail Division implements Regional Vice President organizational structure

Accenture overture prompts Connolly business sale and valuation discussions

2004   **2005**   **2007**

2003   **2005**   **2006**

CCA acquires Finance expertise

Connolly adopts new positioning, "Recovering the Most Money Possible"

Connolly implements formal strategic and financial planning process

Connolly sales reaches $100 mil; employee count reaches 434, up 90% since 2003

Libby Connolly Alexander named CEO of Connolly Healthcare

First Mission Statement: "We Exist To Positively Impact The Profitability of Our Clients"

2007   **2007**   **2010**

2007   **2007**   **LATE 2000s**

Healthcare Division rebranded as Connolly Healthcare

Retail and Corporate Operations Presidents named

Wilton office expands for third time since 2001; employee count is at 800, up another 84% since 2007

$20 mil invested in technology infrastructure annually since 2007

2012

CHAPTER 9

Organizing the Company for Growth

Redefining Our Culture

When things aren't working right, ask yourself or
your team: What's wrong with the org chart?

—Libby Connolly Alexander

From the time Larry and I took over from our father and assumed our role as the company's leaders, change became a recurring constant for Connolly. We had handled the expansion into the commercial, international, and healthcare markets. We had managed a difficult transition from an independent contractor model to an employee-based one. And with Rob's help, we had navigated the crossover from paper-based records and data to the digital world. But for the most part, one thing had remained constant: the way we managed—or didn't manage!—our people.

Although they were now employees, for the most part our principals and audit staff operated the way they had when my father ran the business. You had a single principal assigned to a client and a team of auditors who worked the account. The principal reported to Larry or me but for the most part ran "their" business the way they saw fit. This structure worked just fine when we were smaller, but as we grew, it quickly became unwieldy. In addition to overseeing accounts, our responsibilities

No longer could we wing it the way we had in the past and not risk making a costly mistake.

for corporate activities—HR, finance, sales, marketing, infrastructure, legal—continued to escalate. No longer could we wing it the way we had in the past and not risk making a costly mistake.

Quite frankly, we needed help. We needed to offload responsibilities, and we needed to be educated on how to run what was now a much larger organization. One way to do that was by hiring seasoned, experienced professionals who could not only take the workload off our plate, they could also help us learn what it takes to run a much larger organization.

In 2003, we hired Skip Proctor to be our first senior vice president of human resources. Before he came along, we had tried to manage with a third-party HR company, but the more Connolly grew, the more we realized that we needed to have an in-house executive dedicated to managing that third-party relationship. After two years of doing our best to figure it out on our own, we had to find a seasoned pro to help us make sure we were handling our HR affairs in a way that would best benefit the business.

Then in 2004 we made another major decision when we hired on Kip Ford to become our first chief financial officer (CFO). Kip's job was to improve our financial discipline, strengthen our financial capabilities, and bring a sense of professionalism to our finance function. Given we had run finance ourselves for the first twenty-five years of Connolly's existence, this was a big step forward.

Hiring our first two experienced outside executives to fortify our corporate functions made it evident that Connolly was indeed heading in an entirely new direction. We weren't just adding titles to our payroll; we were adding expertise. We were hiring around opportunity, scaling up in response to demand and responsibility that we were not yet accustomed to dealing with, at least not to this point in Connolly's history.

Now that Skip was serving as SVP of HR, one of his first orders of business was to evaluate the performance of Connolly's workforce. As part of that process, he schooled us on two of the biggest pain points within any company:

- *Fit*—Assigning people to jobs that just aren't a good fit for their current skill set.

- *Capacity*—Piling heavy workloads onto folks until they're spread so thin that they can't perform up to par.

With Skip's help, we quickly realized that Connolly was guilty on both fronts: putting people into jobs where they didn't belong and giving people way too much to do. Many small entrepreneurial companies experiencing rapid growth are guilty of putting bodies in positions just to fill holes, then later on recognizing they don't—to borrow Jim Collins's idea—have the right person in the right seat on the bus. This realization was as eye opening as it was inspirational. From this point on, Larry and I started down a path that would help Connolly to focus continually on our organizational structure and the fit of the actual individuals filling the roles, something we had benignly neglected for the most part since taking over the business from my father. Thankfully, we were already assembling a team of qualified professionals that could help us sort things out.

Over and again, trial and error became one of our best teachers as we made one incremental decision after another about organizational design, roles, and then people. After we figured out the importance of prioritizing fit and capacity throughout the hiring/promotion process, we used that insight to deal with an inflection point that changed a lot for Connolly, especially in terms of our leadership. Of course, there were aspects of our organizational design that worked better than others. For instance, things tended to go more smoothly when we handled intradivisional adjustments like the internal changes we made in 2005, when Connolly moved to a regional vice president (RVP) structure for our retail division. One by one, we scouted top talent and promoted every RVP from within.

The RVPs created more oversight for our principals, which sparked the creation of an official chain of command that allowed us to provide our employees with the management and resources they needed to succeed in their roles. In choosing our RVPs, we searched for individuals who had a reputation for producing stellar results and exhibiting sound leadership skills. The decision became one of the first steps in improving the capacity of the retail division. In turn, it created more bandwidth for Larry and me, while placing us closer to our goal of expanding Connolly's capacity in its entirety.

Conversely, there were a few organizational relationships that seemed to cause us more angst. Another legacy of our independent contractor days was the notion that each of Connolly's divisions could act as its own business entity, handling things like sales, marketing, and financing on its own. Instead, we chose a structure that centralized our HR, finance, IT, and sales and marketing as a shared-service-type model.

Generally speaking, the move was common sense. Thankfully, it mostly worked, and it mostly worked well. Moreover, the decision proved to be efficient from a cost and margin perspective. But it didn't come without frustrations, namely for the leaders of our business units, who wanted more control and autonomy over the resources that supported their division.

For one business unit, most of that tension was concentrated around one specific area: sales. In 2002, we had hired our first ever vice president of sales, Tom Santacroce. His directive was to help grow sales for our commercial division, provide sales support to our retail division (since the majority of our retail business was made up of house accounts), and serve as our watchdog to keep us abreast of rates and contracting. Shortly after, our win rate began to increase, and it was clear Tom was being successful.[21] Then we made another hire in 2003, offering Bob Donohue the opportunity to lead our commercial division. As it turned out, Bob's skill set included a strong propensity for sales, creating a redundancy with Tom that ultimately gave way to a tremendous amount of tension and dysfunction. More importantly, the feud began to serve as a substantial distraction, not only for the division but for the company as a whole.

---

21   Jim Riehl, 2003 year-end sales metrics and analysis, organization recommendation, August 22, 2006.

THE RIGHT SEAT ON THE BUS

The relationship between owners (Larry and me), corporate, and Connolly's business units began to devolve into a culture within a culture, so to speak. Perhaps as a legacy of the days of the principals' independent contractor autonomy, the "field," as we called those outside of headquarters, had a certain animosity toward "corporate." This was exacerbated by our hiring of people we knew, leading associates to coin the term "FOL"—friend of Larry/Libby—to describe the relationships Larry and I had with the leadership and employees that worked closest with us.

The FOL label implied special treatment by Larry or me, which for the most part was far from the truth. Tom was classified as FOL-Libby, and Bob was FOL-Larry. Since I handled corporate at the time, including sales, and Bob was aligned with his field people, who saw corporate as a necessary evil at best, the friction that resulted caused interference in our ability to get things done. That said, I would argue that the real culprit was fit. Bob followed his strength—sales—yet we had him in a leadership operations role. Was he in the wrong seat on the bus?

Whether you attribute it to fit, organizational structure, culture, politics, or simply the market opportunity commercial represented, at the end of the day, the dysfunction of our commercial division led to very poor performance. In the height of that dysfunction, the commercial division only contributed 9 percent of Connolly's sales and gross margins, 25 percent less

Despite the resources and investment in that part of our business over time, commercial struggled to get the traction it was seeking.

than the rest of the business.[22] And despite the resources and invest-ment in that part of our business over time, commercial struggled to get the traction it was seeking. In the end, negative gross margin and EBITDA contribution prevailed while creating tremendous disrup-tion and dissension that spilled over into other areas of the business.

In fact, Connolly experienced many of the same issues long after Tom left the company. It begs the question, When is it time to take a hard look at your organizational structure? When do you need to stop to reevaluate the roles people play in your business and, more importantly, whether or not they are the best fit for that role?

Eventually, there came a time when Larry and I decided that we needed to call in reinforcements. We worked with two separate outside coaches over the course of six years, hoping to identify the best way to solve what had become a major breakdown in trust, not just between us but also with many within the company.

Our goal was to become *one* Connolly, one business operating on a single standard of accountability, starting with Larry and me. We planned to learn as much as we could about handling these sorts of issues so we could set up the business for continued success. Larry and I needed to work through this. We needed to set the example.

As leaders of the company, we knew that our behavior would be modeled by every other employee. We knew people looked to us to exhibit qualities they could learn from, qualities that gave them the confidence to continue working for and with us. Even with all of that in mind, the commercial division seemed to be a continued exception to the rule—an issue that didn't go unnoticed on both sides of the fence and that was the thorn in my relationship with Larry.

To be fair, there will always be trial and error when building a business. Businesses don't come with instruction manuals that tell

---

22   Jim Riehl, organization recommendation, August 22, 2006.

you what to do or when to do it. They certainly don't offer crash courses in hiring the right people for the right roles. Connolly was not perfect in any way, but for the most part, we got it right. Despite a few challenges and the occasional upset, we hired some of the most outstanding, dedicated people I've ever had the pleasure of working with. These people helped us build and drive our business, even in some of the most uncertain circumstances. With their help, Connolly remained a definitive leader in the marketplace for many, many years. It was work—*a lot* of work—but at the end of the day, it was as rewarding for us as it was for our associates.

Each time we faced the opportunity to reorganize, we created a moment for folks to step up to the plate, accept new challenges, and grow professionally and personally. Even as we figured things out, Connolly was known for our bias for internal promotions. We truly believed that investing in our people would pay off. That was another reason why we developed such fruitful, long-lasting relationships with our associates, and it was cause for celebration at our town hall and management meetings. Tenure was regularly recognized and celebrated within the company. To know that our employees depended on us, that they trusted us to help them reach their professional and financial goals, is one of the most gratifying things Larry, Robert, and I can ever take away from our time as Connolly's leaders.

ESTABLISHING OUR POSITION IN THE MARKET

Kevin, the head of our marketing department, recognized that Connolly needed to differentiate itself in the marketplace and define our unique selling proposition (USP). He hired a strategy consultant, Dick Albu, who performed a review on the business in November 2004. Jim Riehl, an experienced Harvard Business School graduate who worked for Dick, conducted a strengths, weaknesses, opportunities, and threats analysis, also known as SWOT, which became yet another pivotal move for our business.

If you can believe it, Connolly's lack of a corporate vision or mission statement were two key findings from the SWOT review. Jim's report included a shocking statement, one we had never even considered: "Connolly has reached a plateau." Those words were an instant eye-opener and a call to action. We needed to define our business for the marketplace, and for ourselves. These changes weren't solely necessary to boost our marketable appeal. Jim made us realize that we desperately needed to perform a self-examination. Defining our mission and strategy was going to benefit every aspect of our business.

Jim also pointed out that "Connolly does not market itself—it only sells." This was something else we didn't fully appreciate until the fact was pointed out. He was also astonished with our client satisfaction and retention rates, astronomical numbers he had never seen on any business in his entire career. This led him to recommend our unique positioning statement: "Connolly is the recovery audit expert who recovers the most money possible, and as a result, their clients are 97 percent satisfied and 98 percent loyal." Jim continued to serve as a consultant to the business, helping us implement not only a marketing strategy but also overseeing the implementation of a financially driven strategic planning discipline.

We fell for the classic consultant "you know you need me" pitch, but when it all came back around, Jim proved to be profoundly important in helping us get around to issues like financial planning and organizing our strategic initiatives. His advice served as an incredibly effective tool for accountability, causing us to focus and resource around things we were committed to as an organization.

I believe this was one of the most important things Connolly did to enable the growth of the company between 2007 and 2012. Jim certainly made an impression on us, and I think Connolly returned the favor, because he was ultimately hired to serve as our senior vice president of marketing and strategy. Our time together proved to be another long-lasting, mutually beneficial connection.

OUR MISSION AND VALUES

Once you've mapped out a plan to prepare for growth and laid the framework to execute your strategy, expect to start doing a lot more delegating, and delegation usually means having more employees to manage. These two realities presented a major change in the way Larry, Robert, and I had been running the business. For years, it was just us. Then we started to expand. This expansion meant we needed to make sure everyone we were bringing on board was clear on what our vision was for how we were going to expand the business and the steps we were going to take to get there. Most of those new hires weren't familiar with us or the industry, and eventually, we noticed a drastic decrease in the intimacy we'd once felt within the workplace.

For a big part of our history, we could still call every person who worked for the company by name. At least that was our reality for many years. Our employees knew us, and we knew them. Every associate understood the things we stood for without the need for elaborate explanation. Our values and expectations were pretty straightforward: produce results, do the right thing for the client, and don't cause disruptions. For the most part, things went pretty smoothly.

In the interim, we had a few things to ponder:

Where was Connolly trying to go?

How did we plan on getting there?

These were the first two things we had to address. Answering these questions would also help us deal with some of the feedback received from one of the counselors we were working with, who was tasked with helping us squash some of the role confusion that had been tripping us up. We knew we needed to do a better job of clarifying Larry's responsibilities and authority and repeat the process for me too. Oh, the aches and pains of becoming a more "grown-up" company! But this was essential for us and the business in order to be successful.

It was a process. In fact, the process became a process within itself, if that even makes any sense. All this feedback sent Larry on a mission about our mission. As exhausting as the ordeal was, it was a worthwhile investment that really paid off for us. Eventually, we outlined the framework of our mission statement, working off the Hedgehog Concept presented in Jim Collins's book, *Good to Great.*

Like the hedgehog who is single-mindedly focused, we asked ourselves three questions:

1. What can we be the best in the world at?

2. What are we deeply passionate about?

3. What is our economic engine?

Once we were presented with the questions, our answers were clear, and we were able to define our mission:

Purpose:

We exist to positively impact the profitability of our clients.

Vision:

- To increase annual revenue at double-digit growth rates.

- To be the best in head-to-head competition.

- To attract and retain the best people in the industry.

- To attract and retain the world's largest and best-run companies as clients.

- To commit to long-term relationships by:

  - Consistently exceeding client expectations.

  - Delivering quality results with minimum negative impact on client operation and relationships.

  - Helping clients improve their processes.

  - Continually introducing new solutions to our clients.

- To execute profitably, and with a smile, while adhering to our nine nonnegotiable traits.

Our Nine Non-negotiable Values (NNVs) framed Connolly's values and focus in the most accurate light. They were as follows:

- Customer Service Focused

- Integrity

- Self-Motivated

- Passionate

- Team Player

- Results Oriented

- Reliable

- Professional

- Boundaryless

Everyone in the business seemed to respond to what we'd come up with pretty well. We turned the creation of our mission statement into a collaborative effort, inviting the entire management team to offer insight while it was being written. And because it was collaborative, it was instantly supported by all of the company's senior leadership, the same people who were now expected to help us embed it in everything we did from that point forward.

> *Connolly's values have defined us since the company's earliest days, when there were just a handful of employees. They are the standards of behavior that are at the core of our success. It's what we expect of ourselves and our employees. As we grow, we must be sure that everyone … everyone embraces those values and lives them each and every day. It's part of our secret sauce. It's why we have off-the-chart client satisfaction ratings and why we have such high client retention rates.*

—*Larry Connolly*

We were proud of our first ever mission statement. We all felt really good about it, and we knew that it captured the perfect blend of where we were back then and where we were headed. But there was one more wrinkle. After we narrowed down and agreed on what our NNVs were going to be, they were just words typed on a piece of paper. They did not have any true value or meaning.

They needed definitions. Rather than have the group take that on, Larry turned to me. He trusted that I would get it right. And I did not take the task lightly. I actually sat down with Kevin and hammered out all nine definitions. Even after circulating the defined NNVs to the group for feedback, very little was changed. We finally reached a point where we could feel good about the way we'd structured our business, allowing us …

To keep growing into the future, to achieve superiority in every aspect of what we do, who we are, and who we do it for, for the long term, all the while staying true to the core values that make Connolly, Connolly.

—*Libby Connolly Alexander*

We realized that we had to do more than train new employees on how to do their jobs. It was time to codify Connolly's mission and values so they could know how to do their job for us *the Connolly way*. In the beginning, the relationships we had with our employees were understood, so we never needed to consider these business essentials. Now that we did not have the luxury of forming those close-knit relationships with every single new member of our team, we needed a clearly defined mission and descriptive values to help us attract and retain the best and brightest in the industry.

Our voluntary employee turnover rate was low, between 5 and 7 percent, and we wanted to keep it that way[23]. In order to make that possible, we not only needed to clarify our mission and values but also align our employees with our vision for the future. Around 2008, we started to focus on creating reward and feedback systems that reinforced the culture that had helped us succeed in the past. We would always say, if there was a performance issue, you could usually connect the problem specifically to one of our NNVs. These changes didn't happen overnight, but this was something we felt strongly about. We stuck with our plans and walked the talk along the way.

One way we implemented our newest ideals was through consultant Gary Markle's Catalytic Coaching performance review system. Initiated by Skip Proctor, these were a series of carefully designed employee review systems we'd oriented around our values.

---

23   Connolly, Inc. corporate presentation, February 2012, page 11.

Essentially, we looked for ways to embed our mission and NNVs into everything we did, allowing them to become the foundation of our every business decision. Once they were established, we really kicked things into high gear. Larry would walk into a town hall meeting with employees and pick somebody out of the crowd. He'd offer them a crisp one-hundred-dollar bill if they could name all NNVs on the spot. He sparked the spirit of competition among our employees while making a point about the importance of embracing our mission and values as the core of their roles.

We printed the NNVs out. We framed them and put them on every wall. We even created wallet-sized cheat sheets so there would never be an excuse from an employee. We oriented all of our communications around these values—within our hiring practices, reviews, cultivation, promotion, and even in making the decision to let someone go. This adaptation went on for a number of years. Mission and values became the major break that helped us redefine our business.

Essentially, Larry and I became students of business. Vistage International, a peer-mentoring membership organization for CEOs, played a major role. First Larry joined a group in Atlanta, and then he encouraged me to join a group in Connecticut as well. Our respective groups were major

> *Essentially, Larry and I became students of business.*

resources for leadership education and problem-solving for us both. I will forever be grateful for Vistage Group CE-3612 and the mentorship I received from our chair, Jack Gelman. Each month, Jack would faithfully ask me, "What are the three most significant business decisions you need to make in the next six to twelve months? What do you need to start, stop, and continue doing?" He kept me focused and faithfully held me accountable to my responses.

I also watched as Larry took the lead on discovering some of the most incredible leadership and business books available. "Larry's books" became a roundtable discussion, not just between us but with the rest of our management team. These titles became mandatory reads, literature we'd come together to discuss, either over a casual business dinner or at one of our employee town halls. Sure, some would roll their eyes at the mention of another "book of the month" standard, such as *Who Moved My Cheese?*, by Spencer Johnson, but I was eager to soak it all in.

I learned something from every book we read, and I really enjoyed it. I took the chance to gather information from the nation's best CEOs and business professionals that had succeeded in the way I wished to succeed. Having never gone to business school, I relied on these books, and the conversations that came from them, to help me become a better leader. Having the chance to run through Larry's books, sometimes even meeting the authors who wrote them—Jack Welch, Larry Bossidy, Ram Charan, David Buckingham, Stephen M.R. Covey—was an incredibly gratifying experience.

Our studies revealed a few key pointers on the importance of having a strong mission statement. We consulted numerous examples as a reference, consciously absorbing the structure and content of each message.

> *The mission statement announces exactly where you are, and the values describe the behaviors that will get you there.*
>
> —*Jack Welch, former CEO, GE*
>
> *Stripped to its essentials, an organization's culture is the sum of its shared values, beliefs, and norms of behavior. Values need to be reinforced, but they rarely need changing.*

—*Larry Bossidy, former CEO, Allied Signal*

Over time, you will have to change what you do and, change how you do it, but you don't change what you believe in.

—*Don Soderquist, former CEO, Walmart*

Working to establish our mission and values was one of the most important exercises we undertook and was instrumental in cementing the Connolly culture as we continued to grow.

A DEFINING ORGANIZATIONAL TRANSFORMATION

Walking you through those monumental years when Connolly did our best to figure it out leads to one major event from 2007. By then, we were already a few years into sorting through several organizational issues. In doing so, the future of Connolly became a recurring topic of discussion. Despite the demands of managing the day-to-day of the business, we had to continuously consider how the markets we served were unfolding and how the competitive landscape was responding. Once again, we received an unsolicited inbound expression of interest from another industry behemoth. This time, it wasn't GE sitting across the table from us, it was Accenture.

Starting in 2006, Barbara Duganier, the chief of strategy for global outsourcing at Accenture, was trying to figure out how to expand their business process outsourcing business via strategic acquisitions. Conversations between us progressed, even reaching the point of establishing valuation ranges for Connolly.

Accenture laid a number on the table that had Larry ready to sell. According to him, $80–90 million was "more money than I need or my kids need." Now that the subject was broached and the idea of selling was firmly planted in his mind, Larry went on to say,

"If Accenture refuses to pay at that price, [let's] commit to selling the company within nine to fifteen months [and] use this time to get our house in order."

So that's exactly what happened. Our Accenture discussions didn't get very far, so we began to implement actions to get the business to the point where we would be better prepared in the event another suitor came knocking.

> *We began to implement actions to get the business to the point where we would be better prepared in the event another suitor came knocking.*

It seemed to make sense at the time. I never felt, for even a single moment, that Accenture would be a good cultural fit for our business, and while I was not as convinced as Larry that selling was the best path, I've always lived by the principle that it's important to have a solid Plan B, an exit strategy. Larry suggested focusing on two strong action plans, so we got to work.

First, we initiated a major leadership reorganization. At the time, corporate operations, healthcare, our budding government business, and parts of retail (Canada and the Midwest division) were all part of my responsibility portfolio. I reported to Larry, who also had several retail RVPs, commercial, and the European division reporting to him. We both believed that, by adding a layer of leadership, Connolly's structure would begin to align with our goal of growing market share while maintaining client satisfaction and retention.

Jim Collins taught us to always put your best people on your biggest opportunities. At the time, John Merrill and Jeff Thomas were two of our top leaders that had potential to contribute much more to Connolly. It made sense to promote John to become our new president of retail and to promote Jeff to become the new president of corporate operations. This move freed my responsibilities even more, giving me the chance to focus most of my attention on Connolly Healthcare.

This was the first time in the history of the business that we'd ever created such roles for these divisions. From an organizational standpoint, it was the best move for us. Our retail and corporate sectors deserved to have dedicated leaders, people solely responsible for their success. It also allowed Connolly to carve out much more defined lines of responsibility to absolve some of the friction between our corporate functions and our business units.

As we continued to push through this major reorganizational move, we soon learned that you also need advisors to see you through the unforeseeable. So the second piece of our action plan was to line up the lawyers and bankers we would need in the event of a transaction.

The old adage is never wait to hire a lawyer until you need one. And you never want to wait until the last minute to find a banker or any other trusted advisor either. It's always best to have your relationships in place so you can strengthen those connections over time. You should always position yourself to be able to get to know the ins and outs of the person you may one day need to call on for help. Chances are, when you need a lawyer or trusted financial advisor, it is a time of stress and uncertainty. This way, you'll at least have comfort and know that you're in good hands whenever you need to call on that professional to represent you. It's easy to dismiss the need to assemble a team of advisors before you need them, fearing that it may be too distracting, costly, or time consuming, but it's an important professional must-do. When we made these major structural changes, our relationships with our advisors were a tremendous resource helping us contemplate our options all along the way.

DRINKING FROM THE FIRE HOSE

Despite the distractions of Accenture and our struggles with the commercial division, the fact was we were doing a lot right. Connolly got bigger—*way* bigger. Between 2003 and 2007, we nearly doubled our employees, going from 229 to 434 associates.[24] A lot was changing, and we were experiencing growing pains, but we were still producing results.

With this latest round of adjustments to our org chart, I was faced with a few direct changes as well. My new title this time became CEO of Connolly Healthcare. To be quite frank, at first this felt like a demotion. I'd grown accustomed to juggling countless tasks at the same time. For years, I had my hands in every segment of the business. This latest restructure repositioned a lot of my duties so I could focus on one of our greatest opportunities, but it was still very new to me.

The experience turned out to be very gratifying, though it demanded a lot from me. There was so much in motion at the same time. Between coaching and counseling and implementation, there was a lot for us to iron out.

We planned, then planned around our plans, and kept adjusting our strategy to try to meet our company's potential to grow. Connolly was met with many opportunities to change. Our Wilton office expanded three times between 2001 and 2011, even with what seemed like a solid ten-year plan when we first moved in. We went from two thousand square feet in Stamford to leasing fifty thousand square feet of class-A space in Wilton. This was a real office! I'd say we came a long way from our brown folding tables.

At the same time, our data centers went through a few expansions

---

24 "Mission Possible 2008 and Beyond" presentation, page 5.

as well. In the five-year period between 2007 and 2011, we invested over $100 million in technology infrastructure to reach nearly two petabytes (2,048 terabytes) of online storage capacity, and over seven hundred state-of-the-art servers[25]. In addition to our Wilton data center, we operated a second data center in Darien, Connecticut, for redundancy purposes, and opened a third data center in 2011 to handle Connolly's expanding core business of processing multi-terabyte data sets. At over three trillion payment records annually, we liked to tell our clients, our transaction processing capacity was virtually unlimited.

It was satisfying to see all our hard work bear fruit. Connolly's positioning, strategy, and technology capability not only helped us attract new business and grow our market share but also enabled us to attract and retain the best people in the industry, talent that was the right fit for what we were building. By the end of 2010, we had almost eight hundred employees and were on a path to double again.[26] At the start of it all, Connolly was just a little company that nobody really knew about. By this time, we were really putting our best foot forward, and our hard work was paying off. Maybe a little *too* much.

We were so focused on execution, on delivering on our promises and holding the line against the competition, that we never assumed that growth could become a hindrance for the company. Year after year, Connolly produced record results, and we continued to staff to take advantage of market opportunities. That is until the day we finally realized that we were drinking from a fire hose. Imagine moving from a "grow or die" mission to grappling with the reality

---

25   Connolly, Inc. corporate presentation, February 2012, page 79; Connolly, Inc. lender presentation, July 2012, page 18.

26   Report emailed from Skip Proctor "2010 HR December and Year-End Highlights," January 17, 2011.

that we might have reached our limit as leaders.

Everything we did in response to the various inflection points over the years was done in blind faith. We called out all our issues, made adjustments, and were rewarded with more growth and more market share. The business was performing. Even after counseling, withstanding candid feedback from our associates, and restructuring the organization to try to meet our needs, Larry and I knew we were reaching the apex of our expertise. Twenty years of a 20 percent average compounded annual growth rate meant we were constantly struggling to keep pace with the growth.

For Connolly to rise to its full potential, there were a few more changes that we needed to make, changes we couldn't identify immediately.

Larry and I had to admit that, if Connolly was going to reach its potential, we needed to call in reinforcements.

Eventually, we reached the point where we had to let our responsibility to the business supersede our need for titles and positions. We promised to perform a service for our clients. We let our values attract staff members who believed Connolly was a company that could help them reach their professional goals. At some point, Larry and I had to admit that, if Connolly was going to reach its potential, we needed to call in reinforcements.

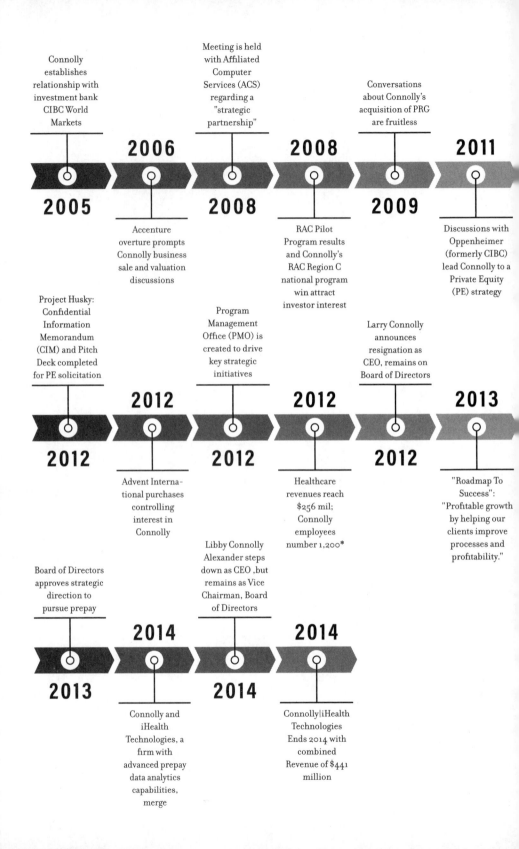

Connolly establishes relationship with investment bank CIBC World Markets

2006

2005

Meeting is held with Affiliated Computer Services (ACS) regarding a "strategic partnership"

2008

Conversations about Connolly's acquisition of PRG are fruitless

2011

Accenture overture prompts Connolly business sale and valuation discussions

2008

RAC Pilot Program results and Connolly's RAC Region C national program win attract investor interest

2009

Discussions with Oppenheimer (formerly CIBC) lead Connolly to a Private Equity (PE) strategy

Project Husky: Confidential Information Memorandum (CIM) and Pitch Deck completed for PE solicitation

2012

2012

Program Management Office (PMO) is created to drive key strategic initiatives

2012

Larry Connolly announces resignation as CEO, remains on Board of Directors

2013

Advent International purchases controlling interest in Connolly

2012

Healthcare revenues reach $256 mil; Connolly employees number 1,200*

2012

"Roadmap To Success": "Profitable growth by helping our clients improve processes and profitability."

Board of Directors approves strategic direction to pursue prepay

2014

2013

Libby Connolly Alexander steps down as CEO ,but remains as Vice Chairman, Board of Directors

2014

Connolly and iHealth Technologies, a firm with advanced prepay data analytics capabilities, merge

Connolly|iHealth Technologies Ends 2014 with combined Revenue of $441 million

CHAPTER 10

The Culmination
of Our Efforts

Change Comes Full Circle

*Decide the values you want to live by, and make them
your true north. It's how you'll be remembered.*

—Libby Connolly Alexander

O ur options abounded. The success Connolly was experiencing caught the attention and interest of investors and experts alike. With so much potential to be extracted from our healthcare division and our best-performing accounts, we knew that we needed to explore all our options before deciding on how to navigate the expansion of the business.

For the first time ever, Connolly had *real value*. But being bigger meant we needed to address certain operational and organizational shifts we hadn't considered in the past.

When we engaged previously with companies like GE and Accenture, we knew Connolly hadn't quite hit its prime. The timing of offers to buy the business (or for us to acquire other businesses) had not quite aligned with our goals. However, with the work of Connolly Healthcare gaining more traction, it was clear we would need to make a few dramatic changes if the business was going to realize its full potential.

More and more, the question was becoming, Do we continue with our growth plan or come up with a different strategy?

Do we buy?

Do we sell?

Or do neither and concentrate on growing organically?

After a number of talks and entertaining various deals, we finally decided to hit the brakes on all possibilities. Rather than allow external forces to control our future, Larry and I thought it was best for Connolly to come up with a strategy of our own. We knew we needed to be *proactive*, not reactive. We grew tired of responding to situations that were initiated by everyone but us. Eventually, we reached a point that forced us to ask ourselves, What do we want to do?

After deciding to knuckle down and map out our future, we determined the timing was right for Connolly to take on a growth equity partner and monetize a part of the business. We needed resources. We needed expertise. We needed insight. We didn't necessarily need the money, but if we were going to lose control, we also thought it best to take some chips off the table. While battling the question of whether we should buy or sell, we had to admit that, quite frankly, we could not answer that question by ourselves. This realization was the big aha moment that led Connolly to form a relationship that would completely shift the future of the business.

PREPARING TO SELL: EXPLORING
THE PRIVATE EQUITY OPTION

Fortunately for us, the relationships we had with our investment bankers began way back in 2005, yielding a trustworthy relationship. While at the St. Mark's Annual May Fair with my children, I ran into my neighbor Ed Eppler as we loaded our kids onto some stomach-churning carnival ride. May Fair is an annual spring town tradition in New Canaan, Connecticut. Everyone with kids goes. With people all around laughing, playing, and enjoying the festivities, the fair became an unlikely backdrop for two dedicated executives to talk business.

At the time, Ed was an aerospace sector banker for CIBC World Markets. The previous fall, PRG had hired CIBC to explore strategic options for the company. Between bites of cotton candy at the fair, Ed suggested Larry, Rob, and I take a meeting with his bank colleagues to talk about our situation and entertain the idea of a potential acquisition of PRG by Connolly. While we passed on that idea, the introduction led to a long and fruitful relationship with the investment banking team at CIBC. Over the course of the next several years, we would meet with these advisors many times to examine all sorts of different transaction possibilities that came our way between 2005 and 2008. Some, like the Accenture scenario, were more seriously contemplated than others, but we knew the stakes were getting bigger with each discussion.

In July 2008, I took a meeting with Affiliated Computer Services Inc. (ACS), another IT and business process outsourcing behemoth who was interested in a "strategic partnership" with Connolly. They had recently won a state Medicaid FFS contract in Florida, beating out another big competitor, and also already had Cigna as a client. Cigna was the only top-ten healthcare payer Connolly could not claim as a client, although not for lack of trying. I never believed in underestimating the competition, so I took the meeting, curious to hear their ideas.

I learned all about the big plans ACS had to consolidate the industry, and I knew they had the balance sheet to do so. Needless to say, they had my attention. I listened on, and while the idea was bold, it became clear that this was another case of an offer about a "strategic buyout," where we would lose complete control and hand over the keys to the business to an entity we did not know. Once again, this wasn't the right solution for Connolly. Thankfully, soon after, Xerox purchased ACS in 2010 for $6.4 billion, and the industry roll up never materialized. In a note to Larry recapping my thoughts about the ACS meeting, I wrote:

The question looms for our $120 million [revenue] company ... Can we continue to compete with an organic growth plan, or does the strategy need to be different?

The question looms for our $120 million [revenue] company ... Can we continue to compete with an organic growth plan, or does the strategy need to be different?

By the summer of 2009, we found ourselves talking to PRG again. This time, the conversation was about taking their company private through a buyout by us and putting PRG's new CEO, Romil Bahl, in charge. Larry was looking for a successor. He was impressed and thought Romil could be the guy, but the price tag was too big, as was the client overlap risk that still existed even after all the years that had passed since our last meeting.

In the fall of the same year, we were having another talk with our bankers, though this time the focus was different. We now realized that, for all the investors and potential partners interested in Connolly, the focus was zeroing in on our healthcare business. Our growth and market share success were not going unnoticed.

The results of the CMS recovery audit contractor demonstration program were public by then, which showcased not only the success of the program but, more specifically, the success of Connolly's contributions. With more than $1 billion in improper payment corrections for Medicare in a little over eighteen months, these reports demonstrated that Connolly could be a successful contractor. This was the proof the industry was looking for, evidence that Connolly was a leader in the recovery audit business, which up to that time had remained cloaked by our deliberate submarine strategy of avoiding tipping off the competition to our success. As soon as CMS released those results, our secret went public right along with the reports.

Based on the success of the demonstration, Medicare expanded the recovery audit program nationally in 2009, and Connolly received a contract for Region C, the Southeast United States and the *largest* of the four contracted Medicare regions. This win caught a lot of attention, and suddenly, we were on the map. From the perspective of the M&A guys, we were a company on the move, and an attractive prospect if you were in the business of making deals.

As the industry carefully examined our results, we were working internally to figure out the best way to manage such tremendous growth. By 2010, we were focused on executing the Region C contract and becoming the number one RAC in terms of returning the most dollars to the Medicare trust fund, a result we ultimately achieved. This opportunity turned 2010 into the first year that Connolly Healthcare surpassed our legacy retail division, although that division was continuing to grow as well. At the same time, we needed to sort out a few lingering issues within our commercial division. To help us move it forward, we hired David Davies in Q4 to serve as the president of commercial, giving him the task of resetting and relaunching the division.

Total company revenue in 2010 went to $158 million from $130 million in 2009, with healthcare growing much faster than any of our other divisions. In addition to our CMS Region C opportunity, our commercial healthcare clients represented over $500 billion in annual paid medical claims. Judging by our revenue plan for 2011, it suggested that Connolly healthcare alone was on a path to $100 million.

In response to what the future seemed to hold for Connolly, many things required our attention, especially within our organizational structure. At the time we had a business where one division was experiencing exponential growth with attractive margins while another, retail, was maturing and in need of margin improvement. A third, commercial, was faltering with negative margin growth despite significant investments. Evaluating all the tasks on our to-do list, 2011 became the year when we admitted we needed help capturing the business's full potential.

With this realization, we ended up hosting a conversation with Oppenheimer (formerly CIBC) to weigh our options. We'd been around the block before, having navigated these waters for seven years and engaged many interested parties in the past. During this discussion, we decided on a solution we felt would best align with Connolly's mission, vision, and values. And that meant going to the market in search for a growth equity partner that could help us realize the potential of the business. The decision, though different than anything Connolly had ever pursued in the past, was the right thing to do for our clients, the right thing to do for our people, and the right thing to do for the company's success.

PROJECT HUSKY

Deal making is treated like a covert operation. To preserve the confidentiality of the process, bankers usually label the projects with some sort of code name. Project Husky became the reference for Connolly's next move. It was the beginning of a new era, and the end of the family business structure we'd carried since my father founded the company in Larry's old bedroom in Rye.

Preparing the company for this project was a process in itself. After contemplating a number of possibilities, we formally engaged Oppenheimer in June 2011 to help us explore investment partners, and then it took more than six months of preparation before we were ready to pitch the business. First, we had to get our financials in order, both historical as well as our five-year projections. Once they'd scrutinized the financials we used to run the company, Oppenheimer required us to do something we had never done before: create divisional P&Ls. This was an exercise in itself and a moment of truth for our business.

Naturally, the margin profiles for our various lines of business

As the division P&L's showed, healthcare was growing and the most profitable division.

were all different. As the division P&L's showed, healthcare was growing and the most profitable division. Retail was peaking and slightly less profitable. The commercial division revenue was flat and not profitable at all. We intuitively knew this, but seeing the numbers in black and white forced us to face the revenue and profitability trajectory of the various segments of our business.

Next, we were asked to assist with the drafting of the confidential information memorandum, or CIM, an important sixty-page document used in pitching the business to potential investors. They would look to the CIM for an understanding of the strength of our financials, why we were a market leader, and how we planned to grow.

Then, we had to create the "pitch deck," a 120-page presentation used to guide our investor meetings. You read that correctly: the presentation describing our business was over one hundred pages and would be presented over and over, each time we met with a different group of investors. Maintaining enthusiasm as we went through meeting after meeting was not easy, but the stakes were high, so we persevered.

The presentations were necessary but also created a lot of anxiety for Larry and me. As a private company, we were sharing information that was previously held very close to the vest and *never* before shared outside of Connolly. Realizing all that this process entailed caused a lot of angst within us. Thinking about the CIM left us worrying about lifting our skirts in a single document, a document that, despite the fancy code names and secrecy, we knew our competitors would eventually see.

Over the years, Connolly had seen our fair share of confidential documents not meant for our eyes, and we weren't naive about what would happen with our CIM. In some ways, we were ready for the world to find out about our business. For a long time, we knew we had been underestimated, and at this point we were less insecure about our competition. We were proud of what the company had accomplished, and no matter how uncomfortable the idea made us, we knew leaks in the investment banking world were inevitable.

Swallowing hard, Connolly braced itself for the inevitability. In fact, part of our preparations included a communication plan, our way of being proactive rather than reactive. Anticipating leaks, we decided it would be best if we disclosed our plans with our clients and employees, as opposed to letting them find out through the media or rumors. Being transparent was a good thing, because sure enough, on January 5, *Merger Market,* "a news service reporting on known and rumored M&A processes," wrote an article announcing, "Connolly Consulting mandates Oppenheimer for sale process, sources say." A few days later, the *Financial Times* wrote an article of their own. Project Husky had been leaked; the world now knew our next move.

All of this activity set the communication strategy we designed in motion. We recognized the need to invite our internal executives and top clients into as much of the conversation as we were prepared to disclose. We assured them of the fact that the partnerships Connolly was preparing to pursue would only strengthen the relationships we had with them.

We tried to steer the conversation toward the many benefits of the partnership we were seeking. We highlighted points like, with Healthcare set to breach $200 million by 2012, we could "benefit from both the financial and intellectual capital of a partner to facilitate the ongoing growth of the business and the diversification of a portion of the family's investment portfolio[27]." Other than that, our intention was to maintain business as usual. We countered the potential perception that we were blindly selling the business by assuring our executives and our clients

---

27   Larry Connolly, *"Financial Times* Status Update," communication to senior staff, January 11, 2012.

that Larry and I would remain on board as the business's leaders.

With the communication out to our clients and company, and the CIM, pitch deck, and our financials roughly in order by mid-January 2012, we were ready to start engaging with potential investors. Based on the initial information shared, approximately twenty-four investors expressed interest. With the help of our advisors, that number was narrowed down to a group of twelve, whom we would then take through our management presentation. This is where we'd cite that 120-page document to educate the investors on the growth, development, and future of our business.

Each one of those meetings lasted over eight hours and involved our entire senior leadership team. Larry would kick things off by giving a company overview of our history, values, and business model. Then it was over to me and Mike Sick for the deep dive on our healthcare business. One of the most important points we had to get across was that the RAC program, of which they had all heard as it was public, was just *one* piece of our healthcare business. Our commercial healthcare business was actually much larger and still had tremendous potential. Our success there had been kept hidden by our submarine strategy.

Talking to prospective investors was very different than the conversations we typically had with clients. Investors' questions were pointed, probing, and detailed, and as much as they were trying to understand Connolly and get to know us, we were trying to get a feel for them as well. Between the dinners and lengthy presentations, these were exhausting engagements, but the real work had not even begun. The diligence phase is where the information exchange and explanations turned up a notch.

We had to manage our time wisely, so we eventually narrowed the group to six "finalists." One investor dropped out, reducing the contenders to a group of five. We had several meetings throughout

April and May, supporting the investors with all they requested and scrutinizing their methods in the process. Keenly focused on the quality of diligence exhibited by each potential growth equity partner, we continued the hunt for a company that could help us professionalize Connolly. We were interested in finding an investment partner who *did the work* and truly understood us—not only our opportunities for growth but our culture and what made Connolly, Connolly. What we didn't want was an investor who didn't do the diligence work but wrote us a big check anyway and then became "surprised" by any aspect of our business after the honeymoon was over. We weren't going to take that risk.

> *What we didn't want was an investor who didn't do the diligence work but wrote us a big check anyway and then became "surprised" by any aspect of our business after the honeymoon was over. We weren't going to take that risk.*

While going through this process, one finalist caught, and *kept*, our attention. That company was Advent International. In writing this book, I came across a case study from Advent, the growth equity partner we ultimately selected, that summed up what made our businesses intrinsically compatible.

> *Advent initially invested in Connolly in 2012, purchasing a majority stake in the provider of technology-enabled recovery audit services. Advent worked with senior management of the family-owned company to support scalable growth in its existing healthcare business and pursued a strategy for building or acquiring additional capabilities for its customers.*[28]

---

28   Advent International case study: Cotiviti, 2019.

Right away, it was clear that Advent valued the same things that had carried Connolly for all these years. Whether the focus was on retail, healthcare, or even building up commercial, our primary focus was always serving the customer, just as our father taught us. Advent had the skill set to help us do a better job of managing our growth and continue to create new opportunities for our clients. Recognizing the opportunities this partnership could create, we gave the green light to move forward with the process.

Advent had described us as a "family-owned operation" that focused on accounts payable recovery audit services before venturing into healthcare. The success we saw with healthcare commercial and government payers, especially the major Medicare contract we acquired while in the midst of our negotiations, made their mission clear: "to make transformative, strategic investments using the Connolly platform."

Connolly had strong relationships with its blue-chip customer base, and adding incremental capability to provide them greater value was crucial.

—Advent International Cotiviti Case Study

Although the company's history was attractive enough for Advent to foresee a profitable future, they quickly made it clear that the work on our end had just begun.

What made Advent stand out was the quality of their diligence. The second round of our deep-dive, in-person diligence meeting was held at the Dolce Conference Center in Norwalk, Connecticut. Without warning, I unsuspectingly arrived at the meeting only to find them there with a small army of over thirty experts from fancy, top-tier consulting firms. This group had expertise in every aspect of our business, including IT, HR, finance, sales, legal, and healthcare. Everyone sat jammed in a room, and as they went around making introductions, all I remember is my head started to spin.

"Who are all these people?" I thought. "My god, Advent has spent a fortune on this meeting! They must be serious about Connolly!"

Mike Sick and I guided the oversized group through the deck we had prepared for the meeting. Advent slid in a last-minute request for a demonstration of our data analytics tools, so I called over to our Wilton office in search of Jim West, one of Rob's initial hires in the data services department, who has gone on to be one of our top health-care division managers. It was all impromptu, but I asked him if he wouldn't mind coming over to the meeting to do a demo. No big deal, right? Right. He quickly ascertained the importance of the meeting and the audience. There were only about thirty-plus people waiting to scrutinize him as much as our tools. Talk about stepping up!

Jim, soft spoken but extremely competent, showed up and gave a terrific unscripted demo. I knew he would. He was proud of the tools he'd helped create, and his authenticity gave the large diligence team the view into our technology they were looking for.

Overall, the amount of work Advent did on the company, and the way they went about getting it done, left us with a good feeling about choosing them as our growth equity partner. When compared to the other offers on the table, their proposal didn't present the most immediate value of the three finalists, but we ultimately felt Connolly and its stakeholders could achieve more and we would collectively create more value with them over time. Boy, did we get that right!

In June 2012, Advent purchased 82 percent of the company, with the remaining 18 percent retained by the Connolly and Alexander families. Project Husky was unveiled through a formal announcement about our deal with Advent. We published a public press release that explained our partnership to the rest of the world, calling Connolly "a leading provider of technology-enabled recovery audit services in the United States, Europe, and Canada."

As CEO, Larry went on record to say, "We are extremely excited to announce our partnership with Advent International, one of the country's most experienced private equity firms. Advent has invested in Connolly for its outstanding people, cutting-edge technology, and best-in-class client roster. It is our belief that Advent's significant financial capital and experience will facilitate the ongoing growth of the business, most notably in the healthcare sector."

Just like that, it was official.

It's interesting to think back to our final dinner with Advent, just before we received their official bid. We were sitting in a Norwalk steakhouse that our corporate president, Jeff Thomas, absolutely loved. Gathered upstairs in a private dining room, sweating under the relentless intensity of the late sun in May, we sat at a table just beside a large window in the private dining room reserved for our milestone dinner meeting. Through that window, we had a clear view of the Clocktower apartment building, the place where it all began. The Clocktower was home to our makeshift apartment-office and first ever attempt at a data center. Seeing that image cast over the skyline while we sat at the table, dining with the group that was charged with forging the future of Connolly, was very telling. There we were, twenty-two years later, talking to a group of investors about changing the path of the business forever.

This moment of reflection forced me to think of all that came from our "process" with Advent. There was another time when one of our meetings doubled as a "you can't make this stuff up" moment and a first-time introduction with one of our second cousins, Greg Baumer. He had recently joined Advent as an associate in the summer of 2011, and one can only assume that something transpired that allowed Advent to make the familial connection. They had asked Greg to join the team attending our first ever dinner and to accompany the group to the presentation scheduled for the following day. As we made our way through the usual pleasantries, conversation quickly led to questions about our founder, James A. Connolly, and where he was from. The mention of Scranton, Pennsylvania, was all Greg needed to confirm that our father was, in fact, his great-uncle.

Greg's grandfather, who had passed away at the young age of fifty-four, was my father's youngest brother. This breached the bounds of coincidence—it was absolutely *amazing*! After hearing his proclamation, I did not need much convincing. Upon taking a second look at Greg sitting across the table, I could see that he, my father, and Larry were nearly spitting images. All pleasantries were cast aside as I jumped out of my seat and flew around the table to give Greg the biggest hug that my arms could muster. We never had much contact with this branch of the Connollys. Neither Larry nor I had ever met Greg before, but in that moment, we all felt the immediate connection you only feel when you're in the presence of family.

The experience was nothing less than heartwarming. Tactical or not, Greg wasn't the reason we chose Advent as our partner, but it was nice knowing we had family on the other side of the table, even if he was still in the early rounds of his career. By the fall of 2013, Greg was enrolled at Harvard Business School, and to my knowledge he is the only other Connolly to do so besides my father. I wonder if he took away from HBS as much as my father had promised to teach me, and did, over the years at Connolly.

When you think about the tone of these meetings, you know how rigid and redundant some of them can be. Rows and rows of mostly guys in suits, then me. Everyone's on their best behavior, trying to be charming. It was exhausting! After a few of those, it's easy to see how one could grow tired of the process, but checking out wasn't an option. These were people who would be writing checks for hundreds of millions of dollars, and they were entitled to ask as many questions as they needed to gain understanding. Rather than allow the exhaustion take over, I realized that it was also an important time for me to get to know them on a deeper level. If all went according to plan, I knew I would be trusting those investors with our life's work, and I would soon be working for them. Without a doubt, our meetings with Advent were among the most interesting. Maybe that helped swing the pendulum in their favor, just a smidgen.

TRANSITIONING INTO A PRIVATE EQUITY–BACKED BUSINESS

Private equity, especially growth private equity, seeks to accelerate expansion via investment. After closing on Advent's $715 million investment in Connolly, including a successful raise of $400 million in senior secured credit facilities (a.k.a. debt) in July 2012, Advent wasted no time in helping us map out a plan for us to support scalable growth for our healthcare business. By the end of 2012, all of our projections would prove true, and healthcare achieved yet another record year of growth, with revenue of $256 million, and the company as a whole surpassed 1,200 employees.

The transformation that took place once Advent was involved was fast and furious. Seemingly overnight, Connolly was faced with a plethora of changes. The dramatic growth was creating organizational stress, and we needed to develop a strategy to alleviate it. Initially, the plan was focused in two areas: talent acquisition and accelerating our strategic initiatives via the creation of a program management office

(PMO).

Before we could execute, we had to do some reorganizing of our own. Throughout the process, it became more and more clear that the investors we were engaged with were almost entirely focused on our healthcare business. Advent was no different. Shortly after the close, they initiated discussions to orient the business and all of its support functions around expanding our healthcare opportunity.

Advent made a direct request to have all of Connolly's support functions be accountable to me, operating under the healthcare umbrella, so there would be no question over the focus of resources needed to support the healthcare division. They wanted nothing to distract from this opportunity, reflecting their view on how to get the most return for the dollars they invested. This restructure was their way of aligning all of our efforts behind healthcare's expansion.

Advent came into the equation void of any emotional attachment to our legacy nonhealthcare businesses. They respected what Connolly had grown to become through our modest beginning in 1979, but after taking a magnifying glass to every nook and cranny of our company, they made an objective call on the aspects of the business that deserved the most attention.

It can be challenging to accept the idea that everything you knew your business to be over the last thirty-three years would be changing before your eyes.

It can be challenging to accept the idea that everything you knew your business to be over the last thirty-three years would be changing before your eyes. While Advent was not looking to starve the other parts of Connolly, it was clear that they wanted healthcare to be the priority, which meant that, once again, Larry and I would be shifting responsibilities.

Between August and September 2012, Advent initiated an organizational change that yielded dual CEO titles for Larry and me, but with all of the business's corporate functions operating under my direction. I was asked to focus on healthcare, and Larry was given the mandate to either sell or disperse our commercial division, given the lack of its size and profitability profile.

Larry made the announcement of the changes to the rest of Connolly in an email that also graciously announced my new role and responsibilities. He pointed out the outstanding growth Connolly had seen and predicted the business's expansion into becoming a $400 million revenue business in only few short years. It was nice to see the response from our associates, with many of them remarking how proud they were to witness how beautifully the company had grown during their tenure with us. Although I was regaining many of the duties we'd worked to shift from my plate during the major reorganization of 2007, the time I spent overseeing Connolly Healthcare demonstrated to Advent that this was the best organizational course of action, one that would allow them to fulfill their goal to help the business grow and expand.

Then a change happened for which no amount of planning could prepare me.

It was one thing to resume my role as the reporting executive for our corporate functions. Becoming a private equity business presented its fair share of challenges, but I knew they were manageable. However, when Larry announced he was resigning from his role as CEO to pursue a few of his bucket list dreams, I was not quite prepared for such a dramatic shift. Reading his resignation announcement, I delighted in Larry's incredible career with the business.

After coming on board in 1985 as an auditor for our Walmart account, Larry had the pleasure of seeing the business grow under my father's watchful eye, and then his own. During that time, Connolly expanded from a modest business with thirty-five independent contractors and $5 million in revenue to having more than 1,200 employees, 120-plus clients, and earning over $250 million in revenue that year. And during the twenty-two years he served as CEO, Connolly's compounded annual growth rate was an astounding 20 percent. It is safe to say that Connolly grew into a business larger, more complex, and more successful than it had ever been. Even though he was leaving behind his daily responsibility to the business, Larry continued to serve on our board of directors.

At the same time, Jeff Thomas, the president of our corporate division, also announced his retirement. In an instant, the company was without two invaluable contributors to our leadership team. Considering the plan we'd set in place to facilitate the growth of the business, and all the amazingly talented people who were dedicated to helping us execute that plan, as the lone-standing CEO, I had to step up to be the strength and stability the company needed while embracing the many changes birthed from our transition into a private equity company.

Unfortunately, I did not have the chance to benefit from my father's coaching or wise words of advice, but I did have the pleasure of relying on our partner's experience to get us to the next level. From the very beginning, Advent declared that their most likely exit would be through an IPO of Connolly, so they were looking to invest in talent with public company experience.

Steve Senneff was our first all-star hire. He came to us from Nielsen, a research and data analytics company where he was the number two guy under revered CEO Dave Calhoun's talented CFO. Ironically, the Calhouns lived in New Canaan, and our daughters happened to be classmates. Before Nielsen, Dave came from GE and was mentored by Jack Welch. Dave was someone I looked up to and admired, and as fate would have it, his guy was coming to work for me!

Our next hire was Jason Friedrichs, who came to us via Advent. Jason was onboarded to lead our newly formed PMO. Following him was John Vitale, our new SVP of human resources, who joined the team in December 2012. Then, in January 2013, we welcomed Mike Whitehead as the SVP of IT. I love the fact that we were able to promote from within too. Tony Massanelli was promoted to president of retail in July, upon John Merrill's departure. And finally, Jon Olefson joined us in October as Connolly's very first general counsel. With so many skilled key players in place, I had my very own dream team. The shift in the company's energy was actually quite refreshing.

ADVENT'S GAS PEDAL: CALLING IN THE BIG GUNS

Before long, Advent had us hitting the gas pedal. We were moving our own cheese, and our new leaders were helping to profession-alize our legacy approach to running the business. With each new leader, we began performing assessments of the business to determine where we were and where we needed to be in order to support a $400 million revenue organization and beyond. Under Steve's leadership, Adrienne Calderone, our capable new controller, and a small army of fifty or so temporary people successfully made the switch over four months from cash to GAAP accounting, no small feat for a company our size. We also brought HR and payroll in house and created many new roles and organizational structures to support our profitable growth trajectory.

Our newly formed program management office was poised to

act as the accelerator of our growth and performance. The PMO had us hyperfocused on those key strategic initiatives determined to be the most important drivers of growth. We deployed our typical collaborative approach through town hall sessions, and with the help of our expanded leadership team, we identified our biggest opportunities to drive revenue and EBITDA growth.

We staffed each of the initiatives with a dedicated initiative leader and chose individuals who also happened to be some of our most capable talent in the company. They were responsible for driving results and ringing the cash register in the areas we identified as priorities.

Once we got the PMO organized, however, we realized we had two complex initiatives requiring expertise we didn't have in house. With Advent's support, we brought in reinforcements and hired Bain Consulting to help us with a revenue blueprinting assignment comprising two separate initiatives focused on supporting and fueling our growth:

1. Establish a strategic account management (SAM) capability that would help us develop deeper relationships with our clients.

To meet this initiative, we needed to figure out the answers to the following questions:

- *What does the organic growth opportunity look like within our existing client base?*

- *What should the account management organization look like?*

- *For what should it be responsible vis-à-vis the service delivery organization?*

- *What are the overlaps, and how should those be handled?*

- *How should decision rights be allocated?*

The reality was, our accounts were increasing in size, complexity, and demand. In 2010, our four largest clients, CMS, Walmart, Aetna, and UHC, accounted for $270 million in net recoveries. In 2012, these four clients accounted for about $1.3 billion in net recoveries. In a mere two years, net recoveries more than quadrupled. We knew we weren't fully penetrated but needed to discover how much more we could extract from these opportunities.

We knew our audit delivery leadership was stretched, and we believed adding strategic account management resources to partner with them to offer support would help drive sales and deliver greater results. We just didn't know how to do it. Bringing in the pros, rather than following our own path of trial and error, was more Advent's speed. Historically speaking, we usually opted for a "figure it out" methodology. Fortunately, we saw the benefit of Advent's suggestion right away.

Bain not only helped us with organizational design and governance, but they also helped us develop the tools to elevate our new SAM organization. The implementation of SAM was a no-brainer. Once we blueprinted the organic growth opportunity at our largest clients, we discovered, with approximately $250 million in revenue potential to unlock, all we had to do was mobilize.

2. Determine how to expand beyond the core via new products and services.

We knew prepay was where we wanted to focus our efforts. Clients were clamoring for us to help them get out of the "pay and chase" business, where errors were found after they had occurred rather than before. And if we didn't help them, we knew someone else would. We also knew we wanted to take business away from our biggest competitors, our client's own internal recovery teams! I knew it was going to be important to have buy-in on this initiative, so I worked with Bain to design an inclusive process for this part of the engagement that would involve a substantial number of our healthcare leaders.

Bain led the team through a series of workshops and thought-provoking exercises to identify opportunities for growth beyond the services we were already providing. That these assignments surfaced prepay as the top opportunity to explore was not surprising. With everyone in agreement, we deployed Bain to help us size the opportunity and help us determine two objectives: how do we play and how we would win in the prepayment advanced analytics segment.

After four months (and a lot of market research and analysis), Bain validated our thinking about prepay:

"We continue to believe prepay is an attractive opportunity and a strategic imperative for Connolly."[29]

The strategy we agreed on for how we should enter the market was essentially twofold:

a. Buy iHealth Technologies (iHT), a task that earned the code name "Acquiring Apple," as they were the leader in the prepay advanced analytics market, with 35 percent market share.

b. Begin building prepay advanced analytics capabilities at Connolly as a hedge.

We did both. In 2013, the estimated prepay advanced analytics market was approximately a $350 million market expected to grow rapidly at 15–30 percent annually to $1.3 billion by 2018. It was a complementary opportunity that was undeniably attractive, and

---

29   Bain evaluation of Connolly, Inc., 2013.

without Advent's backing, the investment would have been impossible for Connolly to execute on its own.

THE ROADMAP TO SUCCESS

In November 2013, we completed our engagement with Bain, including approval from the board to pursue prepay. While our strategic imperatives were clear, and before pursuing and completing any acquisition, I felt it was important to revisit our mission and lay out a framework for our future. I enlisted the help of Jason Friedrichs, SVP and head of our PMO, to create a plan that would articulate the future of the business. Since Advent's investment in July 2012, the company had experienced a number of changes designed to stimulate growth, and by November 2013 we were on a path to close the year with a 31 percent increase in revenue and a 65 percent spike in EBITDA. Acknowledging this success, all of the change that had taken place, and the product of our strategy work with Bain, I was inspired to create a plan for how to make our company even better. That plan became known as the Connolly's Roadmap for Success.

I was inspired to create a plan for how to make our company even better. That plan became known as the Connolly's Roadmap for Success.

Connolly's current mission statement was over six years old, and we had to ask ourselves, Was it still relevant? Did it effectively capture who we were and who we aspired to be? Did it support our future direction?

The answer to all three was yes, but there was always room for improvement. The Roadmap for Success essentially allowed us to simplify our mission, adding elements encompassing the direction in which Connolly was headed. It was an evolution of Connolly's mission statement, a refined design that captured four forward-looking growth objectives:

- Retain and build our core business

- Add new clients to grow

- Launch new products that redefine our industry

- Invest in people and technology

Even with all the dealings we were entertaining behind the scenes, the Roadmap for Success was a very deliberate strategy, one that would allow our business to continue to evolve in alignment with our core values regardless of where the future would take us. Anyone who would join Connolly, either a new employee or an entire acquisition, would be able to view our Roadmap for Success as the defining underlying motivators that described the "Connolly way."

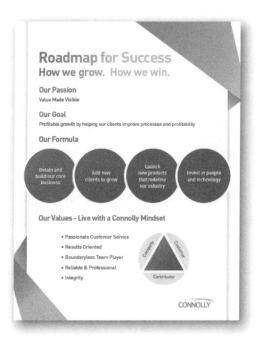

Our goal became "profitable growth by helping our clients improve their processes and profitability," which did not stray too far away from our original mission statement. We developed a plan that would inspire our employees and executives to "live with a Connolly mind-set," which meant being a boundaryless team player, reliable, professional, results oriented, and passionate about the service we offered our clients.

When we rolled out the Roadmap for Success, we explained to our team that integrity was the key to success, a truth that had carried the Connolly business for decades. The Roadmap for Success taught us to look at success as an interchangeable term that honored the needs of the customer, the company, and the contributors—all of Connolly's associates. I wanted our associates to view the roadmap like Connolly's success wheel. When driving a car, having balanced, aligned wheels makes your ride so much smoother. That was the same effect I hoped the roadmap would achieve. The business was already performing well. I looked at the roadmap as a means of keeping Connolly in perfect alignment.

I knew we were actively working behind the scenes to acquire iHealth, but it was very important that any future changes were tempered by the original vision we had set for Connolly. With the knowledge and apprehension that even more change was imminent, I went forward with introducing the roadmap at our 2014 managers' meeting.

Over the years, our brand came to represent something much more than a traditional recovery audit business. We were a professional family that held a vision that promised to uphold the best interest of all those who placed their trust in us. Despite the changes that lingered on the horizon, my integrity would not allow me to ignore this one last move that would keep our business on track for the future we planned for ourselves.

Soon after the roadmap was rolled out, Advent was closing in on the iHT deal, and before long we were sitting down with iHT leadership, talking about the potential of the combined company. Five months later, the merger of iHealth Technologies and Connolly was announced on March 31, 2014.

The merger was a singular move that targeted many of the strategic initiatives detailed in the Roadmap for Success. It meant we could expand our core business, add new clients, invest in people and technology, and launch new products that redefined our industry. Of course, many of our associates had questions about the merger, so I decided to lean back on our most faithful communication strategy: transparency. I held a call with our team to address the most pressing questions anyone would have in this situation, the who, what, and why.

First, who is iHT? They were a leading provider of software-based healthcare recovery audit solutions focused primarily on prepayment, the very area we were looking to venture into. With their help, clients of iHT were able to benefit from being assured of payment accuracy *before* provider payments were released, a completely different segment than our postpayment specialty. In 2013, iHT led the advanced analytics prepay market with roughly a 35 percent share, having reviewed $70 billion in claims in 2013 alone. Based out of Atlanta, iHT was founded in 2001 and, at the time of our merger, had a thousand employees, roughly 250 based in the US and 700 in India.

Answering the who helped make more sense of the why. Not only did iHT create exceptional results on their own, their mission directly aligned with our long-term strategy for profitable growth. Their technology would allow us to fulfill our desire to help our

clients improve their processes and profitability. Combining the pre-
to postpayment services would give us the opportunity to deliver
an end-to-end payment integrity solution that could redefine our
industry. Our healthcare clients were demanding to move away from
"pay and chase" and instead find as many errors as possible *before*
they happened, rather than after.

Initially, I believed this merger would not create much of an
organizational change for Connolly. With Advent's backing, we were
acquiring iHT, and I was under the impression they would become
an independently operating subsidiary of our business. Then I was
faced with yet another monumental change. Companies can't have
two CEOs, a professional truth we all know. However, as a part of
getting iHT's agreement to an acquisition, Doug Williams, iHT's
CEO, requested, and I agreed, that Advent make him the combined
company's CEO. I would step down and shift my focus to serving as
the vice chairman of our board of directors. Part of what led to this
decision was my making it clear I was not interested in running a
public company, and Advent was already headed toward taking the
new company public. While this wasn't exactly how I saw myself
exiting the company after thirty years, I knew stepping down was
the right decision for the business, so I did not hesitate to prioritize
Connolly, as I had for the last thirty years.

On June 4, 2014, I addressed the company for a final time at
an all-hands meeting broadcasted out of Atlanta, Georgia, to all
of Connolly and iHT's employees worldwide. Following the town
hall, I led my last board meeting as CEO. My year-to-date update
said it all:

> *2014 started off extremely strong for all segments of Connolly
> … Q1 Revenue was $83.5 million, 44 percent YOY growth
> and $6.2 million favorability to budget. Q1 adjusted*

EBITDA of $30.2 million is 185 percent over 2013 and $5.7 million favorable to budget. Healthcare grew 60 percent YOY; retail grew 13 percent. Along with outstanding performance and continued execution on our strategic initiatives, one of the largest wins YTD was successful diligence and deal closure with iHealth Technologies.

—June 2014 Board of Directors Meeting

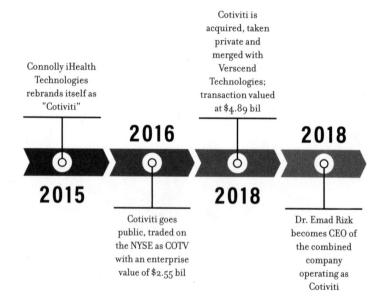

Connolly iHealth Technologies rebrands itself as "Cotiviti"

2016

Cotiviti is acquired, taken private and merged with Verscend Technologies; transaction valued at $4.89 bil

2018

2015

2018

Cotiviti goes public, traded on the NYSE as COTV with an enterprise value of $2.55 bil

Dr. Emad Rizk becomes CEO of the combined company operating as Cotiviti

Building the Future by Reflecting on the Past

W hen I realized that Advent was very committed to the idea of launching an IPO as the best strategic action for them and the business, I had to be honest with myself. I abhorred the idea of spending the better part of each quarter ramping up for big presentations and conference calls on our financial performance. I detested the thought of having to face the inevitable barrage of questions from "the Street." I had gained enough exposure to the capital markets through our multiple debt raises and refinancings to understand investment of time was required and was a necessary evil. Still, I had spent thirty years being heavily involved in shaping our strategy, developing relationships with our clients, building teams, and working alongside our people on all the aspects of the business, and that was what I loved the most.

Working on strategy, meeting with our managers, teams, and clients, was what made the job so exciting and engaging for me. Through our clients, I had a front-row seat with some of the world's largest and most impressive corporations.

We had many clients who were direct competitors in cutthroat industries with distinct cultures and approaches. This made our work both challenging and interesting. In May 2014, I foresaw how being a public company CEO would considerably take away from the role I had learned to love and cherish. I always tell people to find their "true north," and for me, being a public company CEO just didn't line up to my personal expectations. Rather than hold onto a role that I was not 100 percent committed to, I recognized how influential iHealth's CEO could be in that position. My love for Connolly would not allow me to cut ties entirely, however, and although I formally announced my intention to step down, I remained on the board of directors and continued to contribute to the company's success.

What we accomplished over the years was nothing short of remarkable. During my time with the business, I had the pleasure of witnessing our company's continuous evolution, as well as my own. Coming from my background as the modest history major working at the World's Fair to ultimately representing our business as its proud CEO, this experience was truly fulfilling. Although I went through more than a few role changes over the years, I was always committed to supporting the business where and when it was needed.

Without accruing major debt or biting off more than we could chew, our calculated methods helped us expand globally and enjoy a hard-earned leadership position in the markets we served. After bravely entering the healthcare sector—knowing nothing about paid medical claim auditing—we fought our way to become the market leader in that segment also. Many of the goals we set began as nothing more than curious ideas. We followed our hunches, trusted our instincts, and learned from our mistakes—that is what contributed the most to Connolly's success.

We were fearless. Following our father's lead, we never let the absence of opportunity steer us away from bravely creating our own path. I spent thirty years building and learning to lead a growth business. You can learn a lot about how to navigate different climates during that time. Reflecting on those three decades of experience, the following is a summary of a few prominent life lessons I learned and highlighted in this book.

Risk taking—Take risks, but make sure they are calculated risks or deliberate risks versus taking a flier based on hope and then calling it a "calculated'" risk after the fact. Calculated risks are about being thoughtful about why you are taking the risk, what you are hoping to achieve, and why you think your goal is possible.

Reflecting on those three decades of experience, the following is a summary of a few prominent life lessons I learned and highlighted in this book.

Points of pain are almost always ailments in the org chart—When things aren't working right, ask yourself or your team what is wrong with the org chart. Pinpoint the pain point. It usually has something to do with something not working right in the org structure.

Instincts—Everyone generally has good instincts, but you have to be willing to listen to yourself or your inside voice (your own Gazoo!) when it's talking to you. I know I haven't listened to mine when I have said something like "I knew that was a bad idea" or "I knew we shouldn't have done that" or "I had a feeling that wasn't going to work out."

Be willing to make "no go" decisions—Some of the best decisions I have made in my career were *no* decisions. In general, it's easier to say yes rather than "no, bad idea, we are not going to do that!"

Organic growth—I've never been a big gambler, and I don't believe in making big bets. If you have a big idea, start small, prove the concept, and figure it out. I call that cracking the code. Once you crack the code, scaling is easier, and you're in a better position to go all in.

Strategy—When a new idea or direction emerges, you need to consider *up front* how public you want to be about your plans. A submarine strategy isn't necessarily natural for an organization but can help establish market traction, making it difficult or even impossible for the competition to catch up.

Competitive paranoia—Pay attention to your competitors. They are better than what you or your team would like to believe. A healthy dose of paranoia is a good thing and will help you keep your edge. I am a mother of four, so it's natural for me to worry, and I'm always worried about the competition. There is always someone out there who is better, always!

Listening—The best new ideas for making money at Connolly came from the people who have worked for the business. Put yourself in a position to hear what they have to say, and be smart enough to listen, no matter what their title is or where they sit in the organization. I love the town hall format for this purpose.

Leadership—When you grow up in your own business, you realize leadership is something you need to work on. No one gave me an instruction manual on how to grow and run a business. One of the reasons I think I have been successful is that I try to have an open mind. It's hard, but I realize that I don't know what I don't know, and I'm willing to work on it. Self-awareness is really important.

Change—Leading change takes courage. Leaders need lots and lots of courage to leave the known behind and lead in new directions. It's simply hard to put emotion and the past aside to move an organization forward, but it's the only way, and that's why it takes courage.

Culture—Culture is a reflection of the values of a company and its leadership that authentically supports and cultivates those values. Companies can't manufacture culture; its leaders need to be authentic and walk the talk.

Reputation—It's true that you can spend years building reputation and lose it all in a single action. Do the right thing when no one is looking; it's as straightforward as that. Never compromise your personal integrity if you care anything about your reputation.

Legacy—Change is constant and can be fast paced on both professional and personal fronts. You *can* be that guy or gal who gets smacked with the impossible, that something that's never supposed to happen to you. We are all vulnerable to this possibility, so keep in mind that life has a beginning, a middle, and an end, no matter how long you live. Decide the values you want to live by, and make them your true north, as that is how you will be remembered.

Customer relationships—They truly are the number-one priority, and it's all about trust. We all have customers. You need to take care of them, and they need to be able to trust that you will deliver above all else. If you don't have customers who trust you, you've got nothing.

If you don't have customers who trust you, you've got nothing.

During my time on the board, from July 2012 to August 2018, I witnessed as the business took on many new projects related to data analytics and organizational initiatives intended to help the new company grow. In 2015, the business changed its name to Cotiviti to bring together the Connolly and iHealth brands under one umbrella prior to the IPO. Cotiviti went public on May 25, 2016, listed on the New York Stock Exchange as COTV, with an enterprise value of approximately $2.55 billion.

By 2018, Advent was in the sixth year of their investment in Cotiviti, still owning roughly 50 percent of the company. After some discussion, the board determined that the best path for the business was to run a new process. In August of that year, Cotiviti was sold to the private equity firm Veritas Capital, then merged with Verscend Technologies, a leader in data-driven healthcare solutions and a Veritas Capital portfolio company. That same month, Cotiviti was taken private in an all-cash transaction and delisted from the NYSE. The transaction valued Cotiviti at $4.892 billion or 17.9x LTM as of March 31, 2018. Dr. Emad Rizk became CEO, and the combined company is operating under the Cotiviti name.

I am proud to say that I was able to play a major role in the growth of such an amazing company. Though the change was plentiful, and the challenges constant, I am honored to have had the opportunity to position my family's legacy business so that we could defy all odds and achieve remarkable feats, all while we continued to grow, win, and deliver for our clients and employees.

We had figured it out.

CONNOLLY US REVENUE

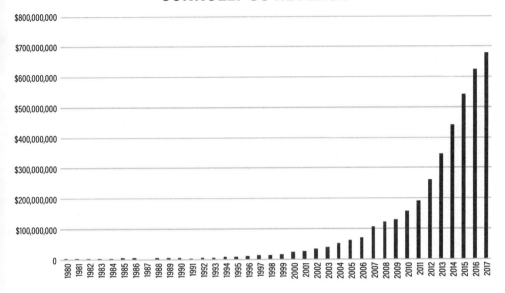

CONNOLLY
PHOTO
JOURNAL

James Aloysius Connolly,
Lieutenant (SC) USNR

The *SS Platano*, a Central American banana ship recommissioned as a supply ship of the US navy auxiliary assigned to provision ships in Amphibious Group 12 during the Second World War

TIME

U.S. SHOPPING SURGE

Trendy Bloomingdale's

Trendy Bloomingdales
"The seventies were the
decade when Blooming-
dale's came into its own."
—Marvin Traub

People and Business

Connolly Named Gimbels Head

James Connolly has been appointed president and chief operating officer of Gimbels New York, which operates the Greater New York area. 10 department stores in He had been vice president and treasurer of Bloomingdale's operated by the Federated Department Stores chain.

In making the announcement yesterday, **Martin S. Kramer,** chairman of Gimbel Brothers Inc., the parent company, said Mr. Connolly, who is 55 years old, would be responsible for all phases of control and operations of the New York division. He succeeds **Matt Kallman,** who was elevated recently to chairman and chief executive officer, responsible for merchandising and sales promotion.

Mr. Connolly, a 30-year veteran of the retailing business, is a graduate of the Harvard Business School, where he majored in marketing and finance.

James Connolly

the French civil service, he succeeds the late **Jacques Chaine.** . . . **William L. Lurie** and **Donald P. Brennan** elected executive vice presidents of the International Paper Company, effective Sept. 1. . . . **John A. Hardin,** president of the First Federal Savings and Loan Association of Rock Hill, S.C., will become president of the United States League of Savings Associations at its annual convention in New York City in November. . . . **David F. Lewis** has been elected president and executive committee member of the Blessings Corporation. . . . **John E. Sumter Jr.** has been appointed chairman of the credit policy committee of the American Security Bank. . . . **Thomas J. Coates** and **Christopher L. Skillern** have been appointed vice presidents of Bank of California.

CLARE RECKERT

later announced there would be no supports until the suit had been resolved.

The suit was brought by

2-Year Treasury Notes

New York Times, Friday,
August 20, 1976

Congratulatory note from former retail executive colleague Howard Schultz, founder of Howard Schultz & Associates, the first recovery audit firm to expand internationally and the leader in the field until the mid 90's

BUSINESS PEOPLE

Connolly Leaves Gimbels New York

James A. Connolly resigned yesterday, effective immediately, as president and chief operating officer of the New York division of Gimbel Brothers Inc., and tongues immediately began wagging in the city's tightly knit retail and apparel communities. The official reason for his resignation, as given in a two-sentence news release, was "to pursue other business interests."

Mr. Connolly, now 57 years old, joined the division (which operates 10 of the 38 Gimbels department stores) as president in August 1976. His departure comes less than a month after Brown & Williamson Industries, a subsidiary of B.A.T. Industries, the British company, established a new retail group to encompass Gimbels, the Saks Fifth Avenue specialty stores and the Kohl department stores.

Mr. Connolly was unavailable for comment yesterday, but Elliot J. Stone, chairman and chief executive officer of Gimbels New York, called the resignation "a mutual parting of the ways that didn't happen suddenly." In a telephone interview, he said that Mr. Connolly "now wants to do something different, and we want at the same time to run this business with a little different structure."

A retailing veteran with more than 30 years' experience, Mr. Connolly was responsible for the control and operations functions at Gimbels. Previously he had been vice president and treasurer of Bloomingdale's, owned by Federated Department Stores, and had served in other Federated posts.

Mr. Connolly's resignation follows the retirement on Jan. 29 of Martin S. Kramer as chairman and chief executive officer of the parent Gimbel Brothers. That was the date that Brown & Williamson made known the major restructuring of its retailing organization and named Allan Johnson, chairman of Saks, and Robert Suslow, president of

James A. Connolly

Saks, to head the new retail group. But Mr. Stone said that yesterday's announcement was unrelated to the January reorganization and termed Mr. Connolly's abrupt exit "merely a coincidence."

Mr. Kramer's position was not filled after his retirement, and Mr. Connolly's will also remain vacant, "at least for now," according to Mr. Stone. Retail observers indicated that Gimbels might be moving away from the tandem system of management now prevalent at the major retailing corporations, whereby a chairman and a president divide the merchandising and operating responsibilities, and might be returning to the older system of one-man divisional management.

New York Times, Feb. 28, 1979

751 Forest Avenue. The Connolly family home where the company was founded in Rye, New York, 1979.

Larry Connolly's graduation from Rye High School, class of 1975

Jim and Connie Connolly
in Rye, New York with
Larry and Libby, August
1977

Larry while a student at Washington
and Lee University, class of 1979

Jim and Connie Connolly with Larry and Libby
at Tulane University

Connolly Consulting Associates early accounting entries in Boorum & Pease Co. ledgers. Examples of manual book entries by Jim, Larry and Libby Connolly

CONNOLLY ASSOCIATES

Sample List of Clients

ABRAHAM & STRAUS Brooklyn, NY	J.C. PENNEY New York	WAL-MART STORES Bentonville, AK
LORD & TAYLOR New York	CERTIFIED GROCERS of Florida	WALGREEN DRUG Chicago, IL
CALDOR Norwalk, CT	ZAYRE Framingham, MA	PAYLESS NW DRUGS Portland, OR
FILENE'S Boston, MA	MONTGOMERY WARD New York, Chicago, Kansas City, MO.	JAMESWAY STORES Secaucus, NJ
I. MAGNIN San Francisco, CA	THE BON Seattle, WA	FREDERICK & NELSON Seattle, WA
NORDSTROM Seattle, WA	THE GAP San Francisco, CA	AMES DEPT. STORES Rocky Hill, CT
KOHL'S DEPARTMENT STORES Milwaukee, WI	BEN FRANKLIN Chicago, IL	LEEWARD'S Elgin, IL
KINNEY SERVICE CORP. Harrisburg, PA	JOHN WANAMAKER Philadelphia, PA	DAYTON'S Minneapolis, MN
CLOVER STORES Philadelphia, PA	MARSHALL FIELD Chicago, IL	PETRIE STORES Secaucus, NJ
EMPORIUM CAPWELL San Francisco, CA	CARSON PIRIE SCOTT Chicago, IL	LECHMERE Woburn, MA
SUPERX DRUGS Cincinnati, OH	GROSSMAN'S Randolph, MA	JOHN BREUNER San Ramon, CA
E.F. MacDONALD Dayton, OH	ECKERD DRUG Clearwater, FL	HOME DEPOT Atlanta, GA
HERMAN'S WORLD Carteret, NJ	ANGEL'S HOME CENTERS Los Angeles & Phoenix	BULLOCK'S Los Angeles, CA
ELDER-BEERMAN Dayton, OH	HANDY CITY/HANDY DAN San Antonio, TX	BUFFUMS Long Beach, CA

Sample list of clients, 1984

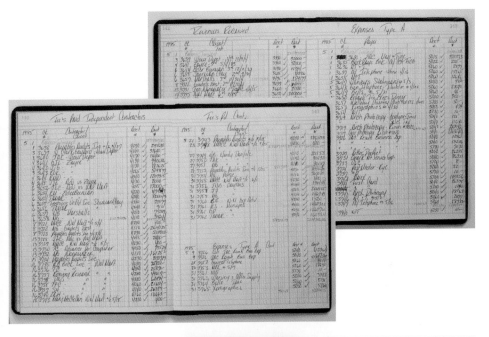

Jim Connolly,
circa 1990

The Connolly family home
in Fiddlers Cove, Cape Cod
- North Falmouth, Massachusetts. Jim Connolly's Pearson
10M sailboat *Tranquility* is
seen at the dock, 1984.

Boxes to the ceiling and brown tables, the Walmart Audit in Bentonville, Arkansas. Libby's first field assignment as Larry's audit assistant, 1986.

Robert in his office at Alexander Systems, 1989

Larry and Libby working in the Clocktower apartment that served as the back office and CCA's first data center, Norwalk, Connecticut, 1991

Father and daughter, Libby (pregnant with Aaron) and Jim Connolly, June 1992

Family portrait taken in honor of Jim Connolly's seventy-fifth birthday at the Connolly family home, Falmouth, MA, Cape Cod.

Larry and Libby Connolly, the new leaders of Connolly Consulting

Original computer equipment comprising Connolly's data center, circa 1994.

Cover of CCA's Qualifications Presentation to Unitedhealthcare marking Connolly's entrance into the healthcare sector, June 1998.

In 2011, Connolly established a third data center in Norwalk, Connecticut, adding capacity to process 3 trillion transactions annually.

The IAPP was all about presence and oneupmanship forcing investments in trade show booths, sponsorship and entertainment. This was our first "custom" booth unveiled in the early stages of our grow or die strategy, 1998.

IAPP 1996, CCA's first trade show booth. L-R Larry Connolly, Bob Lancaster and Dick Van Pelt

Connolly's client-prospect event at the IAPP conference in Dallas, Texas hosted in the newly opened Cowboys Stadium, 2010.

Connolly's leadership team post our 2007 defining organizational transformation.

Back Row: Tom Santacroce, VP Business Development; Jeff Thomas, President Corporate Operations; Jim West, VP Data Services; Bill Wivel, VP Retail & International; Kevin Clark, VP Marketing; Tom Mohs, VP Audit Operations; Skip Proctor, SVP HR; Bob Donohue, EVP Commercial
Mike Matloub, VP Technology; Jeff Goldsmith, RVP Retail & Canada
Tony Massanelli, RVP Retail; Kevin Guy, VP Commercial; Margie Koller, SVP Healthcare; Julius Alexander, EVP Government Services
Kip Ford, CFO;
Front Row: Mike Sick, President Connolly Healthcare; Libby Connolly Alexander, CEO Connolly Healthcare; Larry Connolly, CEO Connolly Inc.; Robert Alexander, CIO
Missing: John Merrill, President Retail; Jim Riehl, SVP Marketing

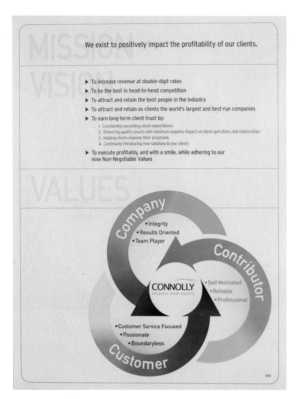

Poster of Connolly's first mission statement exhibited proudly in every Connolly office in the US, UK, and Canada.

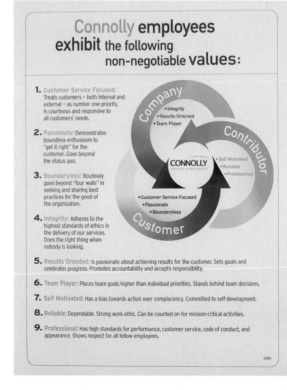

Poster of Connolly's nine non-negotiable values exhibited proudly in every Connolly office in the US, UK, and Canada.

Anchored around our mission and values, Connolly named multiple times one of the 25 best workplaces.

1: Mark Johnson; 2: Libby Alexander; 3: Robert Alexander; 4: Larry Connolly; 5: Jeff Lohmeyer; 6: Kevin Guy; 7: Bob Donahue; 8: Emilio Garcia; 9: Warren Welch; 10: Unidentified; 11: Denise McFarland; 12: Gina Milito; 13: John Lang; 14: Margie Koller; 15: Kevin Clark; 16: Lee Hircock; 17: Dave Brady; 18: Denton Jones; 19: Lisa Irwin; 20: Tony Massanelli; 21: Bob Beckman; 22: Chuck Argo; 23: Tom Magnotta; 24: Mike Sick; 25: Rick McLaughlin; 26: Curtis Rayer; 27: Steve Miskiewicz; 28: Virginia Crawford; 29: Dave Lancaster; 30: Mike McGauley; 31: Joe McGee; 32: Jeremy Bamford; 33: Lori Aronson; 34: Neil Miller; 35: Ed Miscencik; 37: Tom White; 38: Kip Ford; 39: Larry Jeanette; 40: Jon Daniels; 41: Martin Drake; 42: Chad Janek; 43: Bob Miron; 44: Deb Jenkins; 45: Dale Engen; 46: Jonathan Lewis; 47: Jeff Goldsmith; 48: John Heighway; 49: Peter Dovey; 50: Scott Gallentine; 51: Butch Jones; 52: Anna Ramsley; 53: John Sturmer; 55: Jim Riehl; 56: Bob Serocki; 57: Tom Fisher; 58: Chris Gearheart; 59: Tom Santacroce; 60: Jason Pluenneke; 61: Stan Parker; 62: Karen Fejta; 63: Brad Neilson; 64: Rich Schalabba; 65: Howard Flaum; 66: Ryan Mooney; 67: Jim West; 68: Glenn Hall; 69: John Kennedy; 70: Brian Travers; 71: Luke Jasper; 72: Herb Baron; 73: Mike Matloub; 74: John Merrill; 75: Marilyn Foddrill; 76: Tom Mohs; 77: Sunil Raihal; 78: Karl Erickson; 79: Kevin Scott; 80: Mark Irwin; 81: Steve Crabbe; 82: Dan Duggen; 83: Paul Benson; 84: Bill Lawrence; 85: Jeff Thomas; 86: Bob Peterson; 87: Dan Morressey; 88: Ed O'Brian; 89: Skip Proctor; 90: Melisa Ruminot; 91: Ross Biddle; 92: Joel Sauve; 93: Mike Crowley; 94: Daniel Brownell

Wallet size card of Connolly's NNV's given to each and every employee as a reminder of our company values.

Anchored around our mission and values, Connolly named multiple times one of the 25 best workplaces.

Larry, Libby, and Robert celebrating the selection of Advent International as Connolly's growth equity partner, May 2012.